POLICE OCCUPATION/

KEY THEMES IN POLICING

Series summary: This textbook series is designed to fill a growing need for titles which reflect the importance of incorporating 'evidence-based policing' within Higher Education curriculums. It will reflect upon the changing landscape of contemporary policing as it becomes more politicised, professionalised and scrutinised, and draw out both changes and continuities in its themes.

Series Editors: Megan O'Neill, University of Dundee, Marisa Silvestri, University of Kent and Stephen Tong, Canterbury Christ Church University

Forthcoming

Practical Psychology for Policing – Jason Roach, January 2021

Towards Ethical Policing – Dominic Wood, April 2020

Published

Critical Perspectives on Police Leadership – Claire Davis and Marisa Silvestri, March 2020

Policing the Police: Challenges of Democracy and Accountability – Michael Rowe, February 2020

Miscarriages of Justice: Causes, Consequences and Remedies – Sam Poyser, Angus Nurse and Rebecca Milne, May 2018

Key Challenges in Criminal Investigation – Martin O'Neill, February 2018

Plural Policing: Theory and Practice – Colin Rogers, November 2016

Understanding Police Intelligence Work – Adrian James, April 2016

Editorial advisory board

Paul Quinton, College of Policing
Nick Fyfe, University of Dundee
Jennifer Brown, London School of Economics
Charlotte E. Gill, George Mason University

POLICE OCCUPATIONAL CULTURE

Research and Practice

Tom Cockcroft

P

First published in Great Britain in 2020 by

Policy Press
University of Bristol
1-9 Old Park Hill
Bristol
BS2 8BB
UK
t: +44 (0)117 954 5940
pp-info@bristol.ac.uk
www.policypress.co.uk

North America office:
Policy Press
c/o The University of Chicago Press
1427 East 60th Street
Chicago, IL 60637, USA
t: +1 773 702 7700
f: +1 773-702-9756
sales@press.uchicago.edu
www.press.uchicago.edu

British Library Cataloguing in Publication Data
A catalogue record for this book is available from the British Library

Library of Congress Cataloging-in-Publication Data
A catalog record for this book has been requested

978-1-4473-3704-1 hardback
978-1-4473-3711-9 paperback
978-1-4473-3713-3 ePub
978-1-4473-3712-6 ePDF

Cover design by Andrew Corbett
Front cover image: Getty Images (1088155680)
Printed and bound in Great Britain by CMP, Poole
Policy Press uses environmentally responsible print partners

To Ulanda, Tegan, Leah and Minnah.
With love.

Contents

List of abbreviations

EBP	Evidence-based policing
FMI	Financial Management Initiative
HMIC	Her Majesty's Inspectorate of Constabulary
IPV	Intimate partner violence
KPI	Key performance indicator
NPM	New public management
PEQF	Police Education Qualifications Framework
QAA	Quality Assurance Agency

Series preface

Megan O'Neill, Marisa Silvestri and Stephen Tong

The *Key Themes in Policing* series aims to provide relevant and useful books to support the growing number of policing modules on both undergraduate and postgraduate programmes. The series also aims to support all those interested in policing – from criminology, law and policing students and policing professionals to those who wish to join policing services. It also seeks to respond to the call for evidence-based policing led by organisations such as the College of Policing in England and Wales. By producing a range of high-quality, research-informed texts on important areas in policing, contributions to the series support and inform both professional and academic policing curriculums.

Representing the sixth publication in the series, *Police Occupational Culture: Research and Practice*, by Tom Cockcroft, tackles an important topic in policing research that has generated a great deal of scholarly and professional debate for decades. Through this text, Tom Cockcroft presents these challenging and disparate discourses in an accessible and succinct way to allow both policing scholars and practitioners a route to understanding its main contours and contemporary formats, and its applicability to 'real' policing. Aspects of police work which are examined through the lens of culture include the professionalism agenda, ethics, leadership and the various roles officers can undertake. All of this is contextualised within the wider social, historical and political forces which can come to bear upon policing. Informed by research throughout, *Police Occupational Culture: Research and Practice* provides insight, a greater understanding and a deeper appreciation of contemporary debates in police culture and their relevance for police practice.

Tom Cockcroft is Reader in Criminology at Leeds Beckett University. He has researched and published on a wide range of policing topics, including cybercrime training, the policing of young people and dispersal powers, transformational leadership in policing, the higher education agenda in policing, police professionalism debates and, of course, police culture. His research has included collaborations with the College of Policing, West Yorkshire Police, Europol and the Home Office as well as Bundeskriminalamt (the German Federal Police). His work shows a strong orientation towards enabling evidence-based developments in policing policy, practice and training, and thus he expertly bridges what can at times be a wide gap between the academic and practitioner fields. This book represents Tom's second sole-authored text on police culture, a topic on which he has written extensively.

1

Introduction

A number of years ago, I wrote a book on police culture (Cockcroft, 2013) aimed predominantly (although not exclusively) at an academic audience. When I was originally asked by the editors of the *Key Themes in Policing* series to consider writing another book, I was admittedly a little sceptical of the immediate need for another book in this area. By the time I sat down in earnest to work on the book, sometime later, it had become obvious that, despite my earlier reservations, the policing sphere (and the knowledge that surrounds it) had developed substantially and in ways I would not have predicted back then.

One substantial change has been the degree to which police institutions are working closely with those of higher education. A cornerstone of the current professionalisation agenda, the Police Education Qualifications Framework (PEQF), has meant that academic knowledge about policing now needs to be presented in an engaging way to a much wider audience, and one that will increasingly be representing those who practise policing as well as those who just study it. Recent years have also seen a growth in the number of those individuals who simultaneously both practise and study policing and, having been fortunate to spend time working with such colleagues, I am convinced that their presence provides a refreshing and reinvigorating dynamic and purpose to the realm of police studies. Similarly, it is probably very true to say that my own interests in policing, its culture and the surrounding elements that impact on this area have broadened in recent years, and that my perceptions of these issues have been greatly enhanced through working in closer proximity to those who work in the profession.

At a more fundamental level, I believe that police culture has become a concept of real interest not only to practitioners but also to the strategic direction of policing. New developments in police professionalisation, education and leadership seem firmly rooted in the need to respond to the challenges that are associated with the concept of police occupational culture. For example, recent years have seen the advent of robust discussions about what counts as knowledge in policing between, on one side, advocates of evidence-based policing (EBP) and, on the other, those proponents who seek greater recognition of the role that practice-based experience plays in the knowledge of police work. Such conversations can be taken as firm evidence of the ongoing interest in police culture and of its integral importance to discussions of police strategy and operations.

As the police seek to position themselves to meet the rigours of complex late-modern societies where traditional forms of order, rooted in class structures, community cohesion and socially ascribed identities, are becoming destabilised, there remains a fundamental need for a professional police body aligned to the needs of citizens. This juxtaposition of change and continuity was perhaps the key theme of my previous book on police culture. Where this book offers a slightly different take on this relationship is that it provides not only a focus that aspires to be academically sound but also one that is imbued with a greater appreciation of the 'reality' of police work. This should not in any way be taken to mean that some pertinent areas of study have been left out in an attempt to provide a less challenging read. Instead, the book seeks to tackle wider issues, such as, for example, late modernity and neoliberalism, as I believe, presented appropriately, these are both of interest to a broad audience and crucially, integral to our understanding of the 'reality' of contemporary police work.

While many excellent commentaries on police culture have taken as their starting point a politicised position on the subject of society, policing and police culture, this book has taken as its basic premise a more neutral one that has its roots in this idea of social change. Central here is the idea that the political, social and cultural world within which we situate policing has been subjected to, and is still witnessing, substantial change. This therefore draws us towards a critical appraisal of some of the more traditional ideas of police culture. Not, it must be stated, because they are essentially wrong, but because they have limited application to the world in which we now live. And it is this link between wider forces, some of them unrelated directly to policing, that shape our social worlds and the everyday reality of policing which is where the book finds its central axis. This should not be taken as academic reluctance to let go of abstract and intangible concepts that have little role to play in the world of policing. I wholeheartedly believe that the opposite is true, that we cannot understand the cultural world of the police without an appreciation of the wider cultural, political, economic and social change that, knowingly or unknowingly, shapes all aspects of our lives.

Because of the subject matter, and the way I have decided to tackle it, I hope that the book will raise questions, answer questions and, of course, provoke a range of responses among practitioners and academics alike. Dealing with a somewhat intangible and unmeasurable concept as culture, yet one that at times both guides informal behaviour and provokes formal policy recommendations, is always going to be a fairly messy business. To try to limit the scope for the themes, theories and implications for police work to become intertwined, confused and baffling, I have tried to impose a structure through chapters that will, I hope, compartmentalise and limit the subject matter being presented for discussion at any one time.

Perhaps sensibly, this book begins by exploring the different ways in which we can define 'police culture' and the assumptions that underlie these meanings, before exploring the different academic disciplines and approaches that have contributed to the development of knowledge around police culture. In doing so, my hope is to encourage readers to engage with the contested nature of knowledge in this area or, to be more accurate, to understand that different academic disciplines provide very different focuses to our understanding. While this undoubtedly provides the subject with some of its challenging complexity, at the same time this is what gives the area such depth and, I would argue, relevance. This is followed by a return, in some ways, to what might be considered the traditional concerns of much research in police culture, namely the ways in which police culture becomes manifest at the interpersonal level. The book then moves on from the more orthodox and well-covered terrain of the cultural world of the street-level police officer to the relationship between police culture and leadership. In doing so, it will encourage readers not only to explore the existence of distinct and separate leadership cultures but also to consider the ways in which leadership is viewed as the tool by which we set about reforming the traditional police culture. The next chapter looks specifically at the way in which police culture is related to the particular roles that police officers carry out. It therefore seeks to highlight that cultural variation is very much determined by these different roles undertaken by police officers. This is balanced, in the following chapter, with a consideration of those external factors which, over recent years, have impacted on the world of policing and its cultural dynamics. The final substantive chapter briefly considers some of the key elements drawn from police culture literature that can be utilised by practitioners to enhance their understanding of policing, their practice and the cultural dimensions that link the two.

As a whole, therefore, it is the intention here to provide an account of police culture that is directly informed by evidence, research and policy, as well as one that acknowledges the complexities of both the arena of policing and the societies within which it occurs. Furthermore, it is also my intent to highlight the relevant issues that occur in that territory which falls between these two areas – the realm of the individual police officer.

2

What is police culture?

This chapter seeks to outline the challenges of understanding police culture as a tangible phenomenon relevant to practitioners and academics alike. It will identify and explain existing definitions and present police culture as a contested concept, that is, as a subject with a broad range of interpretations, all of which are, to a degree, dependent on the immediate context within which it is being situated. As a result, it will then encourage an understanding of the concept that will allow readers to identify those areas of resonance between the research and literature and their own professional lives or experiences of real-world policing issues.

Probably the first task of any book of this type is to define the subject of its focus, or, in other words, to explain what it is we are actually looking at. If this were a book on, for example, community policing, one would expect this to be a relatively straightforward task. The author could source some textbook definitions, outline community policing initiatives in action and perhaps find some police policies regarding how best to implement such styles of policing. Police culture is an altogether different kind of concept. It does not describe a model of policing, nor an approach to it. It does not generate specific policies on how to do it correctly or lead to targets or key performance indicators (KPIs) on how little or how much of it we think is appropriate. It cannot, arguably, be measured, and does not exist in a physical or tangible sense. At the same time, the concept is viewed as important enough in its effects to impact negatively in numerous areas of police work, both in terms of the internal effective running of the organisation and in respect of the perceptions of those external communities the police serve. In parallel to this, there is evidence to suggest that, in some ways, police culture has substantial benefits for police organisations. To further complicate matters, for many years the term was one used predominantly by academics drawn from disciplines such as sociology, criminology, social policy, law and organisational studies, which all adopted slightly different models through which to study police work. Over time, therefore, much academic debate has focused on the relevance (or otherwise) of earlier ways of viewing the concept and critiqued some of the original assumptions that underpinned it. At the same time, this period signalled a growing engagement with the notion of police culture by police organisations themselves.

As the above probably indicates, police culture is an issue or concept in policing like no other. It was discovered (or perhaps, more accurately, identified) by academics but has, over the space of half a century, come to have real importance to discussions about policing at both operational and strategic levels. So what is police culture? At a very basic level, it can be seen as a way of explaining the common values, attitudes and behaviours that are believed to exist among police officers. And, before presenting more nuanced definitions forwarded by academics, it is probably helpful to explain a number of characteristics of the police role, and academic understanding of it, that will help the reader to engage with the assumptions that are integral to any understanding of police culture. These are: the academic origins of the term; the nature of police work; the class-based nature of policing; and the application of law and morality.

Background context to police culture

It is rare that an issue that is so central to, and so embedded within, the police is identified and articulated by professionals from outside the profession. This was, however, the case with police culture. As mentioned previously, however, we should be aware that the academics who traditionally concerned themselves with matters of policing came from a variety of backgrounds such as, for example, law, sociology, organisational studies and the broader social sciences, and it is perhaps safe to say that that all these can be viewed as 'soft' as opposed to 'hard' sciences. In short, by this we mean that the 'hard' sciences are characterised by the scientific objectivity of the natural sciences, whereas the 'soft' sciences are less exact and tend to be more subjective. The distinction here is important. The interest that policing began to hold for social scientists, notably around the mid-1960s onwards, was influenced by a range of factors. First, the timeline was important. The early 1960s saw the birth of the counter-culture (see Roszak, 1995), a major cultural movement that existed until the mid-1970s, which signalled a growing adherence to anti-establishment views and new lifestyles among young people, particularly in the Western world. Second, this emergence of new social movements was paralleled by similar developments, intellectually, within the social sciences. For example, the work of sociologists Peter Berger and Thomas Luckmann (1966) and Herbert Blumer (1969) expounded the value of symbolic interactionism, a constructivist perspective that proposed that 'reality is both revealed and concealed, created and destroyed by our activities' (unknown author, cited in Fairhurst and Grant, 2010: 173). This approach, based on the idea that our realities are created through our interactions with others, laid the foundations of Howard Becker's labelling theory.

Becker (1963) inverted the traditional approaches of most criminological perspectives by focusing not so much on the criminality of individuals and the ways in which this led to interactions with law enforcement agencies. Instead, he focused on how the state, through police use of powers, had the power to attach labels to targeted individuals and the power of these labels to subsequently dictate the future behaviours of these individuals. In keeping with the irreverent mood of this era of modern history, this intellectual concept similarly appeared to reinforce the anti-establishment sentiment of the time. The third and final element to be understood here is that this change in public and academic sentiment in respect of the power of the state, and the ways in which it is exercised, stood in marked contrast to that of the recent past. Indeed, the period that immediately followed the Second World War and that lasted until the early 1960s has been described by many academics as a 'Golden Age' of British policing. This phrase is generally used to explain the high levels of trust between the public and the police, and to signify an era when policing was commonly focused more on the service elements of the role than those of law enforcement.

We should also be aware that police culture is essentially a term that is used negatively, especially when addressed in the context of British sociology. That is to say, British sociologists undertaking research into police culture tended to present the cultural world of police officers as something to be judged as illegitimate or wrong. Such judgements were not made of other occupational groups of workers. For example, in an article I wrote in 2017, I illustrate how, in 1960s Britain, the growing academic discipline of sociology was largely aligned with the British labour movement, which meant that sociological depictions of police work tended to view policing through a lens that highlighted the police as instruments of class repression (Cockcroft, 2017). This is an interesting position as some academics, such as Mike Brogden (1991), have been keen to identify police officers themselves as one group that became victims of the social order. For example, in his 1991 book exploring the experiences of police officers in Liverpool during the inter-war years, he wrote:

> These officers of the Liverpool City Police possessed immense power over the lives of the traditional objects of

public-order police work, the lower classes of the city streets. But they were, themselves, workers in gainful employment, who suffered severe indignities and humiliations at the hands of their commanders. Rank-and-file officers in the inter-war years were no angels in the way they exercised authority on behalf of a smug urban middle class over the people relegated to the bottom of the social pile. However, they were also working men, subject to extraordinary and often perverse demands from their superiors. Policing involved facing both ways. Police officers were oppressed and oppressors. (Brogden, 1991: 1)

If, however, one looks at the work of Huw Beynon and his depiction of the behaviours and values of those employed in the British car industry (see Beynon, 1984, 2011), readers will see a somewhat sympathetic take on the organisational culture of those who work on the factory shop floor. Such approaches are rarely used when sociologists look at low-ranking workers in police organisations. The reason for this distinction to be made in the treatment of different groups of workers by sociologists is the fact that British sociologists have consistently questioned the legitimacy of the police as an institution. In doing so, the challenges of the working lives of those who work in such organisations is generally downplayed at the expense of a narrative that draws on the misuse of those powers afforded to this group of working men and women. As a result, overt biases exist in many of the accounts of policing from which we draw our understanding of police culture, and these need to be recognised from the start.

One of the key features that explains the enduring interest in police culture is the equally longstanding interest in the police as an occupation. Since its formal inception in 1829, with the introduction of the Metropolitan Police Act, policing has stood apart from many other occupations, perhaps because the introduction of formal police organisations usually occurs at quite pivotal moments in a society's development. For example, the British police were formed in the aftermath of the beginning of the Industrial Revolution, a period that signified wide-ranging change to the social fabric of the United Kingdom. Substantial increases in population (see Wrigley, 1990) led to the flourishing of new metropolitan areas and the subsequent decline of traditional rural communities, causing new forms of social disorder to emerge. The population growth that led to the unprecedented expansion of the UK's cities simultaneously heralded the decline of the apprenticeship system (Deissinger, 2004) that had hitherto exerted a degree of control over the working classes. The relinquishing of this upper-class control, combined with concerns over the socially mobile poor leading to disorderly city environments, contributed to a substantial change in prevailing political ideology. Prior to this, the UK had largely adopted a laissez-faire political stance (associated, according to Rawlings, 2002: 115, with the notion of the 'Freeborn Englishman'), which, simply, sought to minimise state intervention in the lives of the populace. The aforementioned factors, of social change and the growing link to perceived disorder, meant that for the first time Parliament legislated for a specific body to ensure social control. Unsurprisingly, given the combination of events and factors that led to their emergence, the British police were unlike any other organisation in their role, outlook and political significance.

The police present a very different form of organisation, not least in that they occupy a problematic position where the rigour of the law meets the idiosyncrasies of human nature. Therefore, while the law represents, at a basic level, a set of expectations of appropriate human behaviour, complexities arise when one tries to apply these abstracted ideas of right and wrong to the context of complex and unpredictable human societies. This issue prompted Paul Bohannan (1965: 33) to note that 'It is likely that more scholarship has gone into defining and explaining the concept of "law" than any other concept still in central use in the social sciences'. The reason for this is the importance of the extent to which the law reflects the concerns of the populations to whom it is applied. Bohannan went on to note that:

> ... if there were ever to be perfect phase between law and society, then society could never repair itself, grow and change, flourish or wane. It is the fertile dilemma of law that it must always be out of step with society, but that people must always (because they work better with fewer contradictions, if for no other reason) attempt to reduce the lack of phase. Custom must either grow to fit the law or it must actively reject it; law must either grow to fit the custom, or it must ignore or suppress it. It is in these very interstices that social growth and social decay take place. (1965: 37)

This quote remains fascinating because of its fundamental premise that the law is, and has to be, out of step with public opinion. Once this principle is understood, one becomes aware of the challenge that is faced by police officers tasked with implementing the law, which is that for many of the situations where the police will apply legal principles, citizens will view these interventions as unhelpful at best and illegitimate at worse. In other words, if one assumes that the law should be a collection of legal principles that fully reflect the values and concerns of those to whom they will be applied, then the law, as it stands, is imperfect. This is but one factor that provides challenges for police officers and from which cultural responses emerge.

Coupled with the difficulty of implementing a set of laws that do not always reflect or respect the concerns of all sections of a given community, we need to be aware that the challenge of applying the law is made even more acute by the notion of discretion. Discretion, the power of police officers to decide to apply, or to not apply, the law in a given situation, means that a degree of flexibility is available to smooth the rough edges of a legal framework that does not account for the individual circumstances of every possible situation. While such freedom is a necessity, it also leads to challenges of fairness and legitimacy, not least around the equal application of the law. As I noted in *Police Culture* (Cockcroft, 2013), the concept of police discretion often jars with the notion of the law as a fairly and equally applied set of controls. Furthermore, while discretion is a central tool in the work of the police, it is, for much of the time, as much a hindrance as a help. There are unquestionable benefits to discretion as a means of giving police officers the freedom to judge the extent to which a given situation would benefit from the legal application of their powers. However, this is countered by the ability for this discretion to be used as a means by which the police can effectively make decisions that are based on prejudicial opinions and attitudes informed, it is often argued, by their occupational culture. As a result of this, the law can increasingly appear to be a somewhat arbitrary tool in the hands of the police. However, the culture of the police, while often viewed as being fundamentally at odds with mainstream values, does have some roots in the values of wider society. For example, John Crank, writing in 1998 about his work with police officers in the US, noted:

> In the heart of every cop is a sense of morality, strong in some and weak in others, but always present.... Cop culture works in large part because cops start out with a common residue of moral values associated with the traditional, small-town that symbolizes mainstream America.... Police culture transforms and unifies cops with a shared perception of social justice. (1998: 43)

In this way, Crank argues that the morality of the social groups from which police officers are recruited combines with the policing world view. Central here, however, is that the two positions are not necessarily dissimilar. And, regardless of the exact source of these values, it is this culture, what Jerome Skolnick termed the 'working personality' (1994: 41), that is seen as informing the outlook of police officers. While much of the early research in the area of police culture tends to highlight its insularity from the norms of wider society, in terms of its impact on unauthorised or corrupt police behaviour, some research again suggests a degree of influence from the outside world. For example, Malcolm Sparrow et al (1990) show how some illicit police behaviour, rather than being a manifestation purely of the police occupational culture, can also in part be a result of tacit public acceptance of those behaviours. In this way, we can understand how Crank's idea of the 'common residue of moral values' (1998: 43) may still manage to influence the way that the police exercise their duties and do so, on occasion, in ways that depart from both the letter and the spirit of the law.

These ideas provide some of the background knowledge that will help contextualise the reader's understanding of police culture. To recap, therefore, issues as diverse as academic developments in the field of social sciences, the link between British sociology and the labour movement, class dynamics, public morality, the under-reach of the law and the discretion inherent to the police role all combine to influence our understanding of the ways in which police officers navigate their particular social worlds.

Defining police culture

At this juncture, it might be appropriate to introduce some definitions of police culture. In a chapter I wrote in 2007, three definitions of police culture were presented to explore the broadness of the concept and to identify the subsequent challenges of developing an inclusive definition (Cockcroft, 2007). These three definitions (from Janet Chan, Peter Manning and Robert Reiner) are presented again before expanding on these with reference to the characteristics of police culture identified by other authors:

> ... a layer of informal occupational norms and values operating under the apparently rigid hierarchical structure of police organisations. (Chan, 1997: 43)

… accepted practices, rules, and principles of conduct that are situationally applied, and generalised rationales and beliefs. (Manning, 1989: 360)

… a patterned set of understandings which help to cope with and adjust to the pressures and tensions which confront the police. (Reiner, 1992a: 109)

… differences between formal policies and informal practice. (Foster, 2003: 198)

… accepted practices that emerge in groups of officers and their shared understandings about the police mission and standards of conduct. (Bacon, 2014: 105)

… the widespread belief on the part of the police themselves that they are primarily law enforcers – perpetually engaged in a struggle with those who would disobey, disrupt, do harm, agitate, or otherwise upset the just order of the regime. (van Maanen, 1978b: 222)

The police, as a result of the combined features of their social situation, tend to develop ways of looking at the world that are distinctive to themselves. (Skolnick, 1994: 42)

It's a Cop Thing. You Wouldn't Understand. (Message on an off-duty police officer's t-shirt, cited by Crank, 1998: 13)

These definitions are both helpful and challenging. They can be considered helpful in that they identify a broad range of elements that constitute the culture, its application or its causes. They highlight the informality of the culture within apparently regimented organisational environments, the presence of accepted world views that influence and shape practice, the ambiguous real-life application of formally prescribed work behaviours, informal ideas of what constitutes the police role and the professionalism with which it should be undertaken, the role of the police in maintaining order and the uniqueness of police culture to the police role. They can, however, be viewed as challenging in that the final comment, pertaining to the slogan on an off-duty officer's t-shirt, identifies the quite real difficulties in understanding the culture as an 'outsider'. This, in itself, poses quite profound questions for any book seeking to explore culture through the use of evidence as the majority of our formal knowledge about police culture has been generated not by police officers but by academics. And while, at times, police officers have been appreciative of the accuracy of such knowledge, at other times they have not. When I proudly announced in 2017, for example, via the medium of Twitter, a new special issue of an academic journal on the subject of police culture, I was roundly criticised by a number of police officers for presuming that I had the authority to understand police culture as an academic. A fair point, and one that reminds us that academics can by no means claim to have a monopoly on incisive and objective analysis of social groups beyond their own.

And while the issue of who is qualified to define and understand police culture provokes necessary debate on the role of the researcher and the potential to misunderstand police work and its cultural orientation, it is but one of several other challenges. One of the key ones surrounds the extent to which police culture can be viewed as a static and inflexible idea that is applied to policing contexts in different eras and in different national contexts. To do this poses problems. Can we successfully apply the above definitions, for example, to the policing of Los Angeles in the 1930s or the policing of England and Wales in the 2000s or the policing of China in the 1960s? The majority of work into police culture has been undertaken in the UK and the US. In doing so, we find that what we formally know (or think we know) of police culture is very much rooted in the experiences of English-speaking liberal democracies since the 1960s. It might, therefore, be the case that these countries have altogether different policing systems (and therefore cultures) than other national contexts or jurisdictions. At the same time, we have to be aware that great differences exist in legal and policing arrangements between England and Wales and the US. These, in themselves, might make it difficult to meaningfully apply the concept of police culture to other national contexts and historical eras. Similarly, it is important to realise that, at a cultural level, the police tend to reflect some of the broader cultural orientations of the working class of the society in which they operate. This gives rise to the rather confusing possibility that a police officer might have, culturally, more in common with those they police than a fellow police officer drawn from a different national culture.

Even when applying the concept of police culture to the relatively safe contexts of contemporary Western countries, we find that the societies of the 1960s and 1970s (which generated much of our knowledge of the organisational culture of the police) are in many ways largely unrecognisable to those of the present day. The widespread adoption of information communication technology, growing levels of fear of crime, the changing configuration of physical communities, changes to work and leisure patterns, and changes to travel patterns driven by globalisation have all impacted on society. In doing so, they have brought benefits and disadvantages, and changed how people see themselves and the world they live in and, of course, changes in how they interact with it. As a result, this causes challenges of crime, security and order for which the police have responsibility. This idea of societal change is, of course, of considerable importance as policing is largely reactive and responds to the challenges presented to it. And to proponents of late modernity (the idea that the last half a century has seen unprecedented change in these ways), the world is now a profoundly different place to that which saw the first investigations into the subject of police culture.

Causes of police culture

It is worth starting by making the point that, while we are focusing here on police occupational culture, such cultures exist in a wide variety of organisations and institutions. One of the ironies here is, of course, that those university staff who study police culture are often steeped in their very own culture of academia that may shape the ways in which they make sense of the phenomena they observe. At a general level, it is possible to say that cultures evolve within and around occupational groups as a response to the specific roles, contexts and challenges that make up particular jobs. An academic might, therefore, operate in a culture where roles focus on teaching, learning and research, where the context is that of higher education and the institutions through which higher education is delivered, and the challenges arise around publication targets, student recruitment and income generation. For police officers, the culture might be driven by roles of law enforcement, community engagement and crime reduction, the context is both organisation- and community-focused, and the challenges revolve around resourcing, prioritising and responding to social issues of crime, order and vulnerability. It is perhaps unsurprising therefore that different occupations and professions see the world through different perspectives, prioritise some values over others and speak and behave in different ways.

Police culture, however, has attracted perhaps more attention than any other occupational culture. This may have occurred for a number of reasons. First, the real power of police culture is seen as residing at the lower levels of the institution. Much of the focus has been on lower-level police officers engaged in routine interaction with members of the public, where supervisory oversight is at its lowest and where discretion is applied to inform actions (through, for example, decisions to arrest or not to arrest). Second, such decisions are often made, because of the very nature of patrol work, by officers of low rank or limited experience. Third, the culture of the police has been seen as a way of explaining police practices that are considered problematic, deviant or illegitimate.

One of the earliest attempts to explain police culture comes from the work of Jerome Skolnick, a scholar who undertook police research in the US. In his book *Justice Without Trial* (1994), Skolnick explains his rationale for such a piece of work, writing that 'I have tried to learn how those who are charged with enforcing criminal law in a constitutional democracy come to interpret rules of constraint – thereby giving these life and meaning – and analyze the practical dilemmas they face' (1994: viii).

Through using the concept of the 'working personality' (1994: 41), Skolnick tried to explain and isolate the factors that contributed to the police having what was seen as a very distinct and particular world view. Where Skolnick's work has real value for those seeking to understand police culture is that he provides a relatively straightforward model through which we can understand why police officers tend to exhibit similar behaviours and attitudes. Quite simply, he identified three broad factors – danger, authority and efficiency. Danger has long been viewed as a fundamental attribute of the police role. However, there is a need to acknowledge the nuanced nature of danger in the police role. Primarily, we need to distinguish between danger in an actual sense and danger in a potential or symbolic sense. While it would be foolish and untrue to deny that policing as a job does not have elements of danger, it is perhaps the symbolic nature of danger in the police role that helps us to explain its contribution to the police working personality. For example, while not every officer's role will bring them into direct risk of physical assault, the training, environment and language of policing all reinforce the danger that is inherent to policing in an abstract sense. Likewise, authority, in the context of policing, provides a pivotal role in separating the officer, ideologically, from members of the public. It is not just that the issue of authority allows officers to apply the power of the law, but that this power differential facilitates a distance between the police and the public that allows cultural differences to become visible. Finally, the factor of efficiency provides the rationale for police officers to succumb to pressure to achieve discernible results or outcomes. In particular, this draws attention to the role that pressure for results has had on the way that police officers have used their discretion in ways that might not be considered acceptable to those outside the culture.

The three factors identified by Skolnick could be seen as being present, individually, in a wide range of occupations. However, the police working personality as a specific construct emerges due to the specific combination of these three factors and the way in which they interact. One of the reasons why it represents a very helpful way of understanding the causes of police culture is that it allows us to identify some of those elements of the job that make it like no other. At the same time, it would be reasonable to suppose that these three factors are common to the police, in some form or other, in all societies regardless of historical or national context. This provides us with a model that could arguably be seen as being applicable, therefore, to a wide range of police forces throughout the world.

What is also of note in Skolnick's work is a position that has become a persistent theme in accounts of police culture, which is that it underplays explanations of police behaviour based on individual orientation. Through this we can see that the concept of police culture tends to reject ideas that see police behaviours, attitudes and values as being rooted in individual disposition or outlook. Previous to the advent of sociological explanations of police behaviour becoming popular (during the 1960s onwards), police behaviour was either described using a 'bad apple' analogy (if the behaviour was viewed negatively) or by referring to the mythology of the 'British bobby' (if the behaviour was viewed positively). These reference points were inherently based on personal characteristics. Cultural understandings of police behaviour, however, seek explanations not in terms of individual personal characteristics but in the role of the police, the police institution's relationship with communities, and the inherent contradictions of the police as a complex organisation. In this sense, police officers act the way they do not because of any inherent psychological dispositions (as pre-cultural accounts suggest) but because of the nature of police work and the structural and cultural characteristics of the organisation that directs it.

We must also be aware that academics tend to focus on the cultural characteristics of the lower ranks. This may be for a number of reasons. Much of the earlier research into police culture was motivated by concerns regarding the professionalism and conduct of officers interacting with members of the public in the community. These tend, by the nature of the police hierarchy, to be lower-ranking police officers. By the same token, the elite or senior ranks were relatively difficult for researchers to access (as is the case with most elites). To a large extent, therefore, our understanding of police culture has been restricted to the lower ranks because of a combination of their role and of the ability of researchers to access and engage with them. There have been two notable exceptions to this, in the work of Robert Reiner's (1992b) *Chief Constables* and Bryn Caless's (2011) *Policing at the Top*. These pieces of work adopt very different frames of reference to understanding the culture of police leaders, with Reiner's more rooted in the tradition of police culture research and Caless's more directly engaging with the idea of leadership. Despite these differences, both succeed in extending our understanding of police leaders by providing insight into a largely closed group of senior officers (Cockcroft, 2019). Taken together, and by dint of the decades that separated their respective works, they provide a startling account of the changes that have taken place in British policing over this relatively short period.

In terms of their 'cultural' relevance, it is fair to say that Reiner's is more explicitly focused on a sociological audience. It also has particular relevance to explanations of what police culture is and how we explain it, especially in that it provides an explanation of the factors that create the 'world view' of the senior officer. To Reiner, the cultural make-up of the chief constable is determined by four factors – 'period', 'problems', 'place' and 'pedigree'. The period of time (or era) in which a senior officer works will have a considerable impact on their outlook. Every era sees the emergence of new types of knowledge and policy, and their application, to the work of police officers, and these are often not developed within police organisations themselves but imposed from external bodies of the state. And while these new approaches, and their influence, tend to ebb and flow over time, for the period that they prosper they create unique situations. They shape conversations about crime, disorder and police response and shape agendas for action both at an operational level and in the minds of the public. In doing so, these historically located ideas impact on what policing is in the minds of those who practise it and have a role to play in shaping police identity.

The problems that a chief officer faces will similarly impact on their outlook. Problems can take a variety of forms, from very localised issues to national crises, from challenges of public order to public finance, from political intervention to public relations. Likewise, the issue of place similarly moulds the behaviours, values and attitudes of senior officers. Many of the challenges that senior officers face are directly related to the type of environment that they police, and different environments will give rise to very different situations. Maureen Cain (1973), for example, highlights the different policing environments of rural and urban areas and of the ways in which these lead to different types of occupational orientation. Finally, Reiner highlights the impact of 'pedigree' or background on the orientation of senior police officers. This is important in that it represents something of a rarity in police culture literature by acknowledging that personal characteristics may have some part to play in determining the cultural outlook of senior officers.

Relevance to police officers

While the above discussion of what police culture is (and why it occurs) will hopefully be of interest to those with both a practical and an academic interest in policing, it would be helpful at this stage to map out the advantages and disadvantages of trying to apply what has traditionally been seen as an academic concept to the work of those employed within the criminal justice system. The concept can be considered as a helpful means by which police officers can better understand the idea of policing, the wider social context within which the police operate, the roles of the police officer and the multiplicity of issues that impact on the ability to deliver effective policing within ever more complex societies and communities. The latter point is crucial.

Policing is not as simple a process as many media depictions might have us believe. The separate tasks that fall under the policing umbrella can be allocated to quite different and often seemingly contradictory categories. The police are, at various times, there to enforce the law, investigate crime, provide a variety of service or welfare-oriented roles, engage in crime prevention initiatives, take an active and wide-ranging role in the communities they operate within and engage in partnership work with public and private sector bodies. Such an array of roles demands that police officers recognise the variety of work they face and appreciate that the values, attitudes, behaviours and language shaped by police culture will have a part to play in how they effectively undertake their responsibilities. This book, it is hoped, will encourage officers to engage in ongoing reflection about the values and attitudes that they, their colleagues and indeed their organisations hold. At the same time, it also strives to inspire officers to understand how police cultures change over time, between roles and between areas. A further aim of the book is that it will promote reflection among police officers about how the cultural elements of their organisations that can promote positive or negative behaviours may also provoke positive or negative reactions among those communities they police as well as within the wider media and the state.

There are, however, some challenges, as indicated above. While the basic premise of police culture is undoubtedly helpful, police practitioners and academics alike would be wise to approach the concept with a degree of caution. The concept has been used in a variety of ways over recent decades. At its best, it is a genuinely helpful tool for understanding how people work in organisations and the ways in which values can bring some groups together and force others apart. Furthermore, it remains an effective tool for understanding the difficulties of implementing changes in complex organisations and for exploring the varieties of relationship that exist between practitioners and their service users.

However, there are also disadvantages. At various times, to myself at least, the concept of police culture has been used for purposes other than for providing an objective and balanced appraisal of the cultural dimensions of the police world. Some research into police work has provided accounts of policing that appear to be based on the primary assumption that policing is inherently, and unavoidably, lacking in legitimacy. While it is difficult, at times, to ignore the sometimes troubled history of British policing in respect of scandals, differential treatment of social groups and unprofessional behaviour, it is also necessary to acknowledge that we can understand police culture more effectively if we look at the whole picture of policing. In 1999 Her Majesty's Inspectorate of Constabulary (HMIC) effectively critiqued the sometimes blinkered form that our reasoning around police culture takes, when it noted:

> The journalistic shorthand that summarises the thinking of operational police officers as being explained by "a canteen culture" is as misleading as it is mischievous. It is acknowledged that the location reference is merely evocative of what is seen as a collective attitude. These very canteens witness the conversations of officers who still see service to all members of the public as an intrinsic part of their vocation. The number of officers who are nominated each year for community awards are part of this same culture. (1999: 29)

Given the often large cultural differences that have traditionally existed between police officers and academics (although it is not difficult to also identify a number of similarities), it is unsurprising that some academic accounts paint a picture of police culture as being 'wrong' or 'alien'. Another challenge arises in that some work into police culture fails to really appreciate the complexity of the job or its culture. These tend to create deterministic accounts that fail to understand or account for differences in police values and behaviour, the broad array of roles that characterise modern police organisations or the propensity for cultural change through the influence of external factors. These issues will be explored throughout this book.

Questions for further consideration

1. Which of the definitions of police culture outlined in this chapter do you feel is most appropriate or accurate? Consider why you feel this is the case.
2. Reflect on the importance, and relevance, of the phrase 'It's a Cop Thing. You Wouldn't Understand' (Crank, 1998: 13).
3. Reflect on the strengths and weaknesses of Skolnick's assertion that danger, authority and efficiency are central to our understanding of the 'working personality' of police officers.

Further reading

Reiner, R. (2010) *The Politics of the Police* (4th edn), Oxford: Oxford University Press [Chapter 4].

Rowe, M. (2014) *Introduction to Policing* (2nd edn), London: Sage [Chapter 6].

Skolnick, J.H. (1994) *Justice Without Trial: Law Enforcement in Democratic Society* (3rd edn), London: Wiley [Chapter 3].

3

The disciplinary context
of police culture

This chapter will explore the framework from which the evidence base for knowledge around police culture has been drawn. In doing so, it will chart the sociological underpinnings of much of the early ethnographic work in the area through to knowledge derived from a range of other perspectives. As a result, studies including those from the socio-legal, historical, psychological and ethnographic traditions will be explored, as will EBP approaches, to allow for an assessment of the different ways in which knowledge is generated in this subject. The opportunities offered by different research paradigms will be identified to allow readers to critically assess different forms of evidence and their use in exploring policing issues.

In many respects, our understanding of police culture has been driven by the subject of criminology. According to the Quality Assurance Agency (QAA) Subject Benchmark Statement for Criminology (2014), 'Criminology draws on a wide range of human and social science disciplines. The subject's theoretical and methodological development reflects the rapid social changes of contemporary society and is responsive to the increasing cross-fertilisation of ideas and methods between the human and social sciences' (2014: 9). It is therefore the case that our criminological understanding of police culture is largely directed by a mixture of research from a variety of disciplinary subject areas. Over time, the boundaries between these areas have become increasingly blurred and the origins of the subject matter itself have become less easy to identify. To complicate matters further, both policing and the subjects and disciplines that seek to explore it have, over time, developed and expanded their range of concern and influence. All this, as detailed in the previous chapter, has taken place against a backdrop of wider social change.

As evidenced in the last chapter, the source of much of the earlier knowledge on police culture was grounded in sociological traditions. Sociology has, according to Alain Touraine (1989), generally concerned itself with understanding three main types of social change. The first is that of the transformation of societies as they transitioned from traditional to modern structures and displayed new economic, social and cultural forms. The second is the study of the increasingly public nature of human life as the everyday lives of people came under scientific scrutiny. The third is the creation of generalised, and international, knowledge about societies. To situate police culture within this framework we would probably do so with reference to the first type of social change. The reason behind this is that academic interest in the police, and their culture, is largely motivated by our interest in understanding the nature of crime and control, and therefore the relationship between the state and the individual, specifically in respect of how these complex relationships have played out since the introduction of the 'new' police in 1829. As mentioned in the previous chapter, sociologists working within the sociological perspective of symbolic interactionism paved the way for Howard Becker's (1963) 'labelling theory', which allowed for new ways of seeing how state agencies had the power to control citizens through the application of symbolic labels. Such processes were not viewed as just limited to criminal justice systems but also applicable to health, education and other contexts. Increasingly, therefore, the starting point for much of the work around police culture emerged from this social scientific viewpoint that saw power as located within social institutions. Correspondingly, the powerless became the key focus for the application of labels by the powerful. A central element of labelling theory, however, is the idea of secondary deviance, that is, the ways in which the application of these labels can influence the future behaviour of those so labelled through the idea of self-fulfilling prophecies. Labelling theories came to be seen as a contributing factor to our understanding of problematic police practices that would emerge in the late 20th century such as, for example, discriminatory use of stop and search powers.

Ethnographic contributions

Sociology provided the impetus for many of the seminal pieces of police culture research, particularly those based on ethnographic research methodologies. Ethnography is perhaps one of the purest forms of qualitative research as it focuses on the subjectivities of human experience as the basis for our knowledge of the world. In its strictest sense, ethnography represents that research which is undertaken by observing how individuals live their lives in relation to their own natural environment. It therefore represents a departure from the more positivist approaches adopted by the natural sciences (such as chemistry and physics), which use experimental methods to test hypotheses surrounding the phenomena they are seeking to understand. Central to this scientific approach is the study of objects and relationships in an environment where the influence of other variables can be controlled. The opposite approach is adopted by those undertaking ethnographic research. Instead, they believe that the key to developing knowledge is the concept of *verstehen*, a phrase associated with the German social scientist and philosopher Max Weber (see, for example, Weber, 1949), and one that advocates an empathetic understanding of our social world. To do so involves understanding how people act in relation to their natural surroundings, and therefore necessitates a very different approach to research, involving the study of people as they undertake their everyday lives. Bronislaw Malinowski, the celebrated anthropologist, captured this sentiment when he wrote, 'This goal is, briefly, to grasp the native's point of view, his relation to life, to realise his vision of his world' (2005: 19). The purpose of this method is not to establish verifiable truths (as is the case with scientific methods) but to understand how groups subjectively understand and experience their social world. For those studying policing and police culture, ethnography involves observing police officers in their natural surroundings and undertaking their everyday roles. A substantial amount of early research into police culture followed this methodological approach, and recent years have seen something of a resurgence in the popularity of police ethnography. For this reason, a thorough overview of the ways in which knowledge generated by this method can support our knowledge of policing is provided in this section.

The work of John van Maanen (1978a) provides us with a helpful commentary on the method of police ethnography. He begins by acknowledging that, while much of our knowledge about policing (and specifically, police culture) has been generated through this method, relatively little is known about the process whereby this knowledge is generated. Furthermore, he suggests that researchers might enter the field of police ethnography with a variety of motivations that might reflect subjective biases. Some researchers, for example, might secretly harbour desires to join the police, according to van Maanen, while others, contrastingly, may hold a more negative view of police work and those who practise it. When describing his own motivation to undertake ethnographic research, van Maanen showed how the existing literature on policing with which he was acquainted did not fully reflect his own negative experiences of interacting with police officers. Similarly, he makes clear how, despite being a subject of public interest, the actual work of the police remained largely beyond the view of the public.

Such factors reinforce the idea that knowledge derived by ethnographic means can very much reflect the subjective opinion of the researcher as it is based on his or her experiences of policing. At the same time, members of police departments might hold their own biases and be untrusting of social scientists, viewing their work as unduly critical of police practice and, in the words of van Maanen, as 'useless and unintelligible' (1978a: 317). If researchers do gain access to the police, they might find it difficult to sufficiently win the trust of the police so that they act naturally enough, while being observed, to make the research worthwhile.

Secrecy, notes van Maanen, also runs deep within the policing organisation, and does so for a number of reasons. The day-to-day operational information that the police deal in is integral to their success and, as such, represents a commodity that needs to be protected. There is a propensity for those outsiders who enter police organisations to scrutinise police practice to be regarded with a degree of distrust. Likewise, secrecy helps to reduce the possibility of police mistakes, poor practice and operational indiscretions, at both the individual and group levels, becoming public knowledge. Van Maanen goes on to describe the very real challenge that ethnographic research often involves a group of people being studied by individuals with a fundamentally different set of demographic and cultural characteristics. Police officers have, for example, traditionally been seen as holding views to the right of the political spectrum, whereas academics have often been perceived as adhering to left-wing values. Van Maanen also suggests that class differences exist between police officers and academic researchers. Further contextual issues remain. One of these, according to van Maanen (1978a), regards the choice of which police department a researcher should choose to conduct their research within. He states:

> To an observer, the implied differences can be bewildering. There seems to be such an acknowledged diversity of approaches to policing that finding a "representative" department is an impossibility. Even within a given department the variety of tasks performed by various divisions is sometimes astonishing. The police world is partitioned into so many subworlds that it is quite difficult to see any unity of purpose or overall strategy behind police actions. (1978a: 320)

Importantly, those researchers who do get access to a police department after approaching and being turned down by others will never know if the department in which they conduct their research is representative of all the departments they approached or not. For such research, based on one department, the knowledge created is generally that of a case study rather than a piece of research for which the findings can be generalised to a wide body of police organisations. Those departments that have witnessed scandals and subsequent public scrutiny are less likely to open their doors to researchers, and this further impacts on our ability to generate a coherent and consistent knowledge base on policing. Van Maanen, drawing on his own experiences of researching a police department that became embroiled in a scandal six weeks after his research began, noted that the unfurling of such events had a significant impact on how police officers engaged with him as a researcher.

Van Maanen's observations are important. Much of our knowledge about police culture has come from ethnographic accounts, and it is important to recognise that such information, valuable as it is, represents only fragmented perspectives rather than a definitive body of evidence that tells us the 'truth' about policing. Such accounts provide depth and understanding, but make it difficult to come to any real conclusions about policing in a wider sense given the subjective and non-comparative nature of much work. Likewise, there is a concern that pertains to van Maanen's point about the often substantial class and political differences between police officers and police researchers, and this might, at times, lead to very different interpretations of the same events by different people.

Recent years have seen a resurgence of interest in the application of ethnographic method to the area of police studies (see, for example, Loftus, 2009), and this is evident through a collection of new writing on the subject edited by Didier Fassin (2017a). In the introduction to this work, Fassin (2017b) provides an assessment of the challenges posed by ethnographic work and also its contribution to our understanding of our social worlds. First, it is a method which, he notes, asks the researcher to acclimatise to new ways of communication and to accept new social norms, and this requires a degree of learning. Second, it allows us to experience a social environment, through our interaction with other people, that is often very different to our own. In doing so, over time, it allows the researcher to appreciate not just the differences but also the similarities between our world view and that of those we study. Third, through the act of articulating their experiences of the research through their writing, ethnographers are able to provide an inductive understanding of those phenomena they have observed. Finally, Fassin sees the ethnographic method as being applicable to research into all aspects of police activities, making it a very flexible, and relevant, methodological approach.

Fassin goes on to show how police ethnographies provide value as a result of their focus on observation and induction. This allows the ethnographer to undertake a process of 'uncovering' (2017b: 5), whereby inconsistencies between policy and practice (often centred around officers' use of discretion) can be brought to light. Furthermore, ethnography allows for the researcher to go beyond mere observational description and to actually understand the rationale behind observed behaviour. Finally, a further advantageous feature of police ethnography, according to Fassin, is its ability to assist us in 'discovery' (2017b: 6), whereby, through the often monotonous and repetitive tasks that characterise police work, often surprising and novel insights can be made.

Further recent ethnographic work has elicited important knowledge in respect of our understanding of policing in terms of both the macro level, the micro level and, indeed, the interplay between the two. Research conducted by Elif Babül (2017), for example, shows how education has emerged over recent years as a central means by which police reform is achieved. In Turkey, where she undertook the research, education was viewed as essential to facilitating the professionalisation of the police, increasing their effectiveness at crime reduction and of ensuring that police practice meets both domestic legal standards and that enshrined in human rights legislation. Police officers who undertook educational programmes, however, raised concerns that the new expectations were unlikely to be met given the depleted resources, high workload and lack of administrative staff that characterised Turkish police organisations. Through this piece of research, Babül found that the professionalisation agenda essentially sought to standardise police practices as a means not only of facilitating greater accountability but also of increasing police power. In Turkey, Babül concluded, the professionalisation process has, somewhat perversely, reframed police violence as a legitimate technical act rather than a culturally driven and deviant form of misconduct.

Similarly, recent ethnographic work conducted by Steve Herbert (2017) recognises that police officers' behaviour is directed by a range of 'legal, bureaucratic, and cultural systems' (2017: 29) that lie beyond their sphere of influence. Police actions are, he suggests, very much directed towards social situations and environments that are caused by structural factors beyond the police's control. Herbert therefore notes that '… officers neither generate those tensions nor can they remedy them' (2017: 30), and this poses real issues for the application of accountability to individual officers. In doing so, it contextualises police actions less as acts of individual will but as choices derived from a narrow range of options, none of which provides lasting resolutions to social issues. As a result, it positions police officers as relatively powerless actors operating within a flawed social structure. Further examples of the impact of such forces are presented by Susana Durão (2017), who uses the ethnographic study of policing in Portugal to explore new ways of framing the concept of police discretion. In particular, Durão uses ethnography to show how the use of discretion has been impacted by the recent emergence of professionalisation agendas that have led to what officers described as, according to Durão (2017: 236), 'the politics of the numbers'. This refers to those quantitative performance indicators that increasingly influence how the police undertake their ascribed roles. Here we see officer actions, based on individual discretion, largely driven by managerial expectation rather than, as was often supposed, cultural imperative.

Similarly, recent ethnographic work from Mozambique (Kyed, 2017) has shown how attempts at police reform (as a result of concerns regarding police violence) have led to new initiatives aimed at bringing the police and the community closer together. However, rather than reducing the use of physical force by the police, it has actually led to violence being undertaken by civilians on behalf of the police, leading to a hybrid form of control that sits between state oppression and community vigilantism. This is significant in that it provides a means of challenging the view that a closer relationship between the police and the community will lead to more legitimate policing, raising as it does the issue of police-sanctioned community violence.

Finally, Fassin (2017c) focuses on the mundane reality of much police work that stands in contrast to many popular fictional representations of policing. In particular, he explores the relationship between reality and expectation against a context of the 'unending weariness' (2017c: 271) common to both police officers and ethnographers. The officers he studied filled their time by discussing their private lives, current events and their profession. In terms of the latter, their stories balanced their mythologically embedded crime fighting role with their increasing disillusionment with the real-world mundanity of much of their working lives. Importantly, such work reflected the challenges of balancing the myth of police work with the reality, against the backdrop of a culture that sees action and excitement as of central symbolic value. In doing so, Fassin shows not only how there is a cultural explanation for police boredom but that boredom itself has consequences for police action, not least when that boredom prompts officers to take more proactive measures.

As we can see from the above descriptions of police ethnographies, while not without flaws (in respect of their subjective and time-consuming nature and their limited applicability to other police populations), they allow a broad range of police activities to be studied and for new knowledge about culture to be generated. To Fassin (2017b), the resurgence in the popularity of police ethnography is a result of its growing legitimacy within the discipline of criminology. This has come largely as a result of a growing perception that police ethnography has encouraged researchers not only to reassess our theoretical knowledge of the police but also to consider how we understand the lives of those who actually undertake police work.

Socio-legal contributions

The work of Reza Banakar and Max Travers (2005) provides a helpful overview of socio-legal research and its ability to generate knowledge about police work. As its title suggests, socio-legal research refers to social research undertaken by those seeking to understand phenomena through a legal, as opposed to a sociological, framework. In doing so, it prompts the question of whether we can be totally sure as to the exact way by which we differentiate between socio-legal research and sociological research. Many socio-legal researchers, note Banakar and Travers (2005), simply adopt the research methodologies of the social sciences but apply them to more strictly legal subject areas. While the inter-disciplinary nature of the study of law has encouraged the socio-legal perspective, this perspective differs significantly from the sociology of law. To Banakar and Travers this difference is substantive in that socio-legal researchers, while using the methods of social scientific enquiry, root their analysis in legal language and concepts rather than, as sociologists do, presenting these as problematic.

The work of socio-legal scholars has been instrumental in expanding our critical knowledge of certain elements of police work, particularly those aspects driven by operational concerns of how the law translates into practice. A particularly striking example of such an area is that of discretion. Academics have spent much time trying to understand the ways in which the police exercise discretion (or the ways in which they use the professional freedom implicit in their role) to decide whether to intervene and to apply the law or decide to take another course of action. This has been an area of perennial interest for scholars of police culture as discretion can be viewed as the factor that allows for stereotypes, prejudices and discriminatory values to become realised through police behaviour. Such issues have, for example, been integral to understanding stop and search practices and the ways in which privately held prejudicial views can translate into discriminatory police practices. The socio-legal perspective has proven very helpful to our understanding of police culture, therefore, in that while adopting the research methods common to the social sciences, it does not seek to analyse those findings beyond the legal context. In other words, it retains a close focus on the roles, powers and immediate context of law and legal process (in this example, in respect of policing), without deviating into more abstract sociological territory.

As I wrote in *Police Culture* (Cockcroft, 2013), the works of Kenneth Davis (1969, 1975), Carl Klockars (1985) and Wayne LaFave (1962) have all been instrumental in broadening our understanding of the processes that determine how the law is applied by police officers. And importantly, it is the grounding in legal statute, discourse and procedure that enables such scholars to explain variation in the application of the law in a way that those without a legal background may struggle to do. For example, LaFave's research influenced research into police culture on both sides of the Atlantic by using a socio-legal approach to draw attention to the ways in which police officers tended to utilise a significant amount of discretion in their decision-making. While advocating that such powers were indeed integral to the police role, he nevertheless made a strong case to suggest that we need to explore ways of achieving a similar strength of legal controls with which to control non-enforcement of the law as we have for enforcement of law. It is in this issue of discretionary law enforcement (and non-law enforcement) that socio-legal approaches have provided probably the most utility to those interested in police culture. Klockars's work (1985), for example, furthers the analysis put forward by LaFave. While acknowledging the discretionary powers enjoyed by lower-ranking officers, a point that is reiterated in many accounts of police culture, he goes on to suggest that such powers are also enjoyed by officers in other, less public-facing, roles. Although discretionary powers might become more transparently exercised, and involve more strategic decisions, as one rises through the rank structure, such powers undoubtedly still remain. Klockars concludes by revisiting the point made by LaFave, that, while acts of discretionary law enforcement are subject to controls and oversight, acts of discretionary non-enforcement of the law are not.

Historical contributions

Policing as a formal response to the needs of order in society can be traced back to the Metropolitan Police Act of 1829, with only informal policing arrangements existing prior to this. As a result, policing, both as a profession and as an institution, has a deep history. Historical research has been conducted that provides a helpful 'window onto the past', giving us a lens through which to scrutinise current police practice and issues. In a chapter I wrote in 2010 I provided a case to suggest that historical methods, in particular the oral history method, provide an excellent means of generating knowledge around the cultural issues that pertain to policing (Cockcroft, 2010). In this respect, two classic police oral histories stand out – Mike Brogden's (1991) oral history of the policing of Liverpool during the inter-war years of the early 20th century and Barbara Weinberger's (1995) use of the method to explore the policing 'Golden Age' of the 20th century.

Brogden's work draws attention to the essentially class-based elements of police work. In doing so, he highlights the working-class origins of the police, their poor working conditions and the exploitative relationship with the state endured by those who policed the city. Weinberger's (1995) work differs in that it seeks to explore the idea that there was, during the 20th century, a Golden Age of policing where the police enjoyed the unparalleled support of the public. She concludes that, while the police were by no means immune to issues of corruption and unprofessionalism, such widely acknowledged issues failed to tarnish the positive and appreciate view of policing and police officers subscribed to by the general population.

The oral history approach generates knowledge through the use of in-depth and largely unstructured interviews with retired police officers and holds a number of advantages over other methods. It allows researchers to speak with police officers about issues which, due to their sensitivity, would be difficult to broach with individuals currently serving in the police. At the same time, the interviews tend to be broad-ranging and allow for a large amount of contextual information to be generated. Importantly, as noted in an article I wrote in 2005, the approach tends to generate findings that highlight the complexity of the police role, the difficulties of the job and the array of situations police officers have to deal with (Cockcroft, 2005). In doing so, it tends to depict policing in ways that contradict the sometimes linear and deterministic accounts we are often presented with. Furthermore, it tends to uncover 'hidden history'. Much of what we know about policing is derived from high-ranking sources within the police. For example, the autobiographies of senior ranking officers present a very different policing world than those drawn from oral histories conducted with lower-ranking officers. Through using oral history, we learn a lot about the working conditions of police officers at the lower ranks of the profession. Similarly, the complexity of the police role is made clear and these accounts help us to generate democratic understandings of police work that draw directly on the experiences and recollections of practitioners rather than on the interpretations of researchers observing police work (see Cockcroft, 2005). In other words, police oral histories allow us to counter some of the more simplified accounts of policing that have emerged from research. And, while it is unwise to try and directly compare contemporary and historic depictions of policing, the window on the past afforded by oral history allows us to identify themes that resonate both in the past and the present, and therefore to address areas of both continuity and change in policing. In this respect, Weinberger's (1995) work is particularly interesting as her oral history of 20th-century policing highlights some of the persistent elements of police corruption and malpractice that have been identified in more contemporary accounts. Furthermore, her depiction of the challenges to London's Metropolitan Police brought by the particular conditions of the Second World War portray policing at a time of national crisis, where the tasks undertaken by the police changed immeasurably, even if the values that underpinned their behaviours did not.

Evidence-based policing contributions

Over recent years we have seen a new approach to generating knowledge about policing that has tended to question or even displace some traditional thinking about the relationship between policing and research. Whereas, traditionally, 'formal' knowledge about policing was generated by external bodies scrutinising police practice, often through a framework based on a reformist agenda or academic curiosity, EBP is a wholly different proposition. Cynthia Lum and Christopher Koper (2014) define it as, 'a law-enforcement perspective and philosophy that implicates the use of research, evaluation, analysis, and scientific processes in law-enforcement decision making. This research could cover a wide array of subject matters, from evaluations on interventions and tactics to analysis of police behavior, activities, and internal management.'

EBP has a straightforward set of aims, to adopt scientific methods to generate knowledge to improve the quality of police work. The main proponent, Lawrence Sherman, states that, 'Of all the ideas in policing, one stands out as the most powerful force for change: police practices should be based on scientific evidence about what works best' (1998: 2). Sherman has identified a need to adapt scientific method to provide the impetus for effective real-world change in public sector policing.

In doing so, he draws on the example of medicine as a profession that can be based on a rigorous evidence base. While it would seem logical to assume that medical practice was stringently based on evidence, he notes that, even in medicine, one of the most scientifically rigorous areas of knowledge, practice often deviates from that prescribed by scientific evidence.

Sherman highlights the growing move towards governments, and the public sector in general, operating under regimes more closely aligned to evidencing effectiveness. Increasingly, therefore, much effort is spent trying to assess the most effective ways of working within organisations. Sherman's work here is helpful in that it uses this agenda, of evidencing effectiveness, to signal a coming together of research and practice. As is explored elsewhere in this book, police organisations and higher education institutions (such as universities) are increasingly working as partners, with the result that research increasingly informs practice. That is to say, knowledge generated by research is fed back into the organisation to change the way that police officers work. The reason for this is clear for proponents of EBP. For them, police practice has for too long been informed by subjective and experiential perceptions of 'what works' rather than any legitimate base of knowledge. Crucially, this leads to an array of different practices being used by different officers in different policing jurisdictions. This presents a number of challenges. First, 'best practice' is hard to identify or embed. Second, the public are subjected to a lack of consistency in policing. Finally, those police practices that are based on experience rather than scientific evaluation are likely to be inefficient or ineffective. This suggests, therefore, that practice based on 'experience' (and informed by occupational culture) is less effective than that informed by scientific evidence. Sherman's work summarises this argument pithily by suggesting that 'The mythic power of subjective and unstructured wisdom holds back every field and keeps it from systematically discovering and implementing what works best in repeated tasks' (1998: 4). It is important to note here that, according to Sherman (1998), EBP works in two distinct ways. As we can see from the above, EBP is used as a way of generating and embedding scientific knowledge about the best and most effective and efficient ways of undertaking policing tasks. However, of equal importance is the use of EBP as a means of measuring the effectiveness of the police in implementing practice based on scientific knowledge.

The move towards EBP can be considered to be very much a work in progress. Indeed, it is challenging to envisage what a police organisation might look like that is fully committed to EBP given that implementation, at present, varies greatly. Despite this, evidence suggests, according to Sherman (2013), that real progress has been made in displacing the subjectivity which informed much police practice. Indeed, if, as Sherman notes, 1970s policing could be characterised as being based on the 'three Rs' of 'random patrol, rapid response, and reactive investigations' (2013: 378), by 2012 this situation had changed substantially to one of the 'triple-T', which referred to 'targeting, testing, and tracking' (2013: 379). In particular, it should be noted that these changes suggest a substantial development in the underlying ethos of much operational police work. The 'three Rs' are striking in that they suggest the latter part of the 20th century was driven by a reactive (rather than proactive) motive and uncoordinated patrol. The 'triple-T' approach, in comparison, appears substantially more coordinated and proactive.

At surface level, these changes would invariably draw our attention to their impact on the 'three Es' of 'economy, efficiency and effectiveness'. There is undoubtedly, however, a clinical focus with EBP on developing effective strategic police practice, but there is also a similarly important but less tangible relation to issues of legitimacy. Sherman, the most prominent of advocates for EBP, claims that 'The best test of evidence-based policing is whether it has improved public safety and police legitimacy' (2013: 380). This focus on legitimacy is also addressed by Nick Fyfe (2017), who argues that, while it is common for commentators to suggest that policing's power derives from its relation to the law, we should be careful to ensure that this does not obscure the increasing importance of the scientific basis of policing. The reasoning here is clear. Scientific evidence provides an objective and non-partisan knowledge base on which to establish policing as a profession. In shifting the basis of police decision-making from experience to knowledge, the police can claim legitimacy, a principled rationale for the powers they hold, for their work.

Fyfe (2017) identified further benefits of EBP. As well as enhancing the legitimacy of the police, it can help them to respond more effectively to community issues and, in doing so, reduce crime and increase public safety. Furthermore, the recording of data under an EBP regime will allow more rigorous scrutiny of outcomes and lead to higher quality information being fed into organisational strategy. Fyfe also draws on the work of Lum and Koper (2014) to note that EBP could help to neutralise some of the more challenging elements of police culture, which it is suggested can, in some cases, stifle police organisations' ability to change.

A BBC News article from 2018 provides a helpful example of the way in which EBP works in practice. It recounts how Charles H. Ramsey, a police chief from North America, undertook a ride-along with the Israeli police during a visit to Jerusalem. Ramsey was interested to witness that police officers permanently kept the cruise lights of their squad cars turned on. The reason behind this was that it was perceived both as a deterrent and as a way of making their presence known to the public. On his return to the US he adopted the policy in Washington, DC, and in other cities in which he subsequently worked. Police chiefs in other US cities observed this and adopted similar policies. On Ramsey's retirement, his successor, Rick Ross, put an end to the policy on the basis that the 'cruise light' policy, rather than proving advantageous, disadvantaged the police by signalling their presence to criminals. Rather than either of these positions being based on actual evidence, both were the result of nothing more than speculation. It was not until two years after Ramsey's retirement that a Connecticut police sergeant, Jeremiah Johnson, undertook a randomised control trial to assess the impact of 'cruise lights'. His research was inconclusive, and only showed a significant reduction in traffic stops out of all the permutations of vehicle incidents that he measured (traffic stops, vehicle thefts, vehicle break-ins and road traffic collisions). What is significant, however, is that Johnson is typical of a new type of police officer, from outside the upper ranks, who works with academics and uses academic approaches to utilise scientific knowledge rather than 'tried and tested' approaches to deal with issues of crime and order. Such changes in the orientation of police officers to the knowledge that guides their practice could be viewed as evidence for a gradual loosening of the hold that culture has over their practice.

However, the development of EBP has not always been straightforward, and there have been some challenges identified to balance out the advantages highlighted above. While many academics and police leaders have appreciated the potential benefits of this bridging of scientific method and reason to the world of policing, there has been some resistance from operational police officers who have been reluctant to engage. Likewise, it needs to be noted that scientific opinion is not the only factor influencing how the police do what they do. Compelling external factors such as local and national politics and media reporting on crime and security issues undoubtedly have a significant impact on what gets done in policing. Finally, and importantly, there has been considerable debate over what actually constitutes 'evidence'.

Untangling the relationship between evidence-based policing and police culture

As has hopefully been made clear by the above, EBP presents some interesting issues for our understanding of police culture. In particular, EBP was brought in partly as a response to a perceived negativity towards culturally derived knowledge. Such knowledge was viewed as lacking an evidence base and of encouraging practices that were lacking in professionalism or unhelpful in the context of contemporary community expectations of law enforcement. In doing so, this sets up quite a distinct tension between evidence-based knowledge and experiential (or experience-based) knowledge.

While police culture is often viewed in respect of the machismo of rank and file officers, Jackie Goode and Karen Lumsden (2018) identify how higher ranks display a more nuanced form of such cultural characteristics whereby leadership is seen as synonymous with making 'unreflective on-the-spot decisions' (2018: 81). In other words, the assertive and pragmatic cultural traits of the patrol officer are manifested, albeit in different ways, at senior level. Goode and Lumsden found their focus on police–academic partnerships allowed them to explore a number of relevant areas such as the practical impact of EBP, the contemporary pressures on both police forces and universities, and those factors that lead to effective partnership work. One particularly significant finding of their research was the identification of two ways of understanding police culture. The first, they state, reflects our traditional understanding of lower-level policing practices, that is, the idea of police culture in its simplest and most recognisable form. The second, more significantly, conceives of culture as those practices that emerge from 'organizational structures and processes' (2018: 87). By this, they suggest that police organisations have transformed from bodies seeking professionalisation to those seeking 'McDonaldisation'. This distinction is important in that it suggests that organisations seek no greater level of understanding of their operational outcomes than whether or not they can be loosely categorised as either a 'success' or 'failure'. Such a reductive view of complex police organisations does little to encourage personal or professional development among employees.

This research is important for two main reasons in respect of police culture. First, it highlights that police culture is not just something that occurs among the lower ranks. Importantly, it also suggests that some of the dynamics of police culture also get played out among the higher ranks (in this case, in respect of snap judgements being valued over reflective judgements). Second, it suggests that police culture is, in part, generated not so much through the practices of lower-ranking officers but through the ways in which police organisations are overly concerned with the appearance, rather than the reality, of being efficient or effective. EBP, as we shall see later in the book, not only represents a means of understanding and improving police work but is also a fundamental means by which the scope and influence of culturally informed police practice can be reduced.

Psychological contributions

The subject area of psychology might, at one level, be considered as being not particularly helpful in respect of understanding police culture, as much of its focus lies in exploring phenomena at the individual level as opposed to the group level. That said, it has provided a helpful insight into several areas associated with police culture such as the cognitive elements that lead to prejudicial policing, group dynamics, police officer stress and the ways in which police officers use intuition in their working practices.

Taking as our starting point a focus on racially prejudiced policing, we tend to adopt a position that suggests that the police are to blame due to their 'racial animus' (Song Richardson, 2014: 2962), or alternatively that the fault lies with victims on account of their behaviour towards officers. L. Song Richardson suggests that, while it might be tempting to look for a simplistic explanation that casts straightforward blame on one party or the other, social psychological explanations can help us understand the issue with greater clarity. As a result, Song Richardson draws on a variety of research to suggest that the majority of North Americans hold unconscious biases against African Americans.

In particular, Song Richardson draws on the concept of 'implicit racial bias' (2014: 2962) to help us to understand the ways in which unconscious individual stereotypes and attitudes can impact on officers' work-based practices in a variety of ways, from officer recruitment to the use of first aid procedures at the scene of an accident. Song Richardson identifies two specific forms of implicit racial bias. The first of these is the unconscious association between physical racial features and criminal behaviour that leads to unintended and unrealised racial profiling. The second, 'implicit dehumanization' (2014: 2963), refers to the ways in which white police officers tend to view black people as less human than other racial groups. Importantly here, Song Richardson draws on research that suggests that this process has a measurable impact on how officers undertake their work. The higher the level of dehumanisation, the more likely officers were to have used force against young black people.

In this article, Song Richardson also highlights the related but largely overlooked factor of 'implicit white favoritism' (2014: 2964) that directly relates to the aforementioned issues of racial bias and dehumanisation. While research suggests that officers tend to view non-white racial groups negatively, there is an associated tendency for officers to attribute positive traits and features to non-black groups, and this is viewed as leading to more privileged treatment of members of these groups. While racial disparities in police work are understood to be due to these two parallel processes, the eradication of one will not remove the problem. For example, the removal of racial bias, without the further removal of white favouritism, will do nothing to benefit the quality of police interaction with members of minority ethnic communities. This therefore highlights the real problem of police racism. Police racism occurs even when there is no discernible difference between the behaviour of white and black members of the community, or any conscious racism on the part of the police officer.

Song Richardson continues by examining the relationship between police officers' use of force and their sense of self by highlighting the importance of 'stereotype threat' (2014: 2966) and 'masculinity threat' (2014: 2970). In respect of the former, this refers to the idea that police officers experience stereotype threat when, in this context, they are concerned that their actions will be perceived as racist. Furthermore, it occurs when officers believe that those individuals who are judging them are themselves being disrespectful or are perceived as viewing the police institution as lacking in legitimacy. In such situations, officers are more likely to view themselves as potentially at threat of harm. This, in turn, makes it more likely for police officers to engage in violent behaviour. Masculinity threat, in contrast, refers to those concerns that men experience when they believe they may not be viewed as sufficiently masculine. This can lead to overt displays of masculine behaviour as a means of reducing the scope of this threat and, in doing so, lead to violent behaviour. This 'hypermasculine police culture' (2014: 2973), as Song Richardson describes it, is important in that it highlights the more individual elements of what we often conceive as a group organisational culture.

Peter Ainsworth (2002), like Song Richardson, describes the ways in which psychological concepts can help us to understand the group dynamics that we often refer to as police occupational culture. In particular, he explains how new recruits make sense of a complex organisational world by categorising their world into a range of 'types'. In doing so, new recruits look for ways of facilitating this process, and often seek to engage with other people to help them in this process of defining their work-based world. The work of Leon Festinger, and in particular his social comparison theory of 1954, shows us how, when faced with such choices, people often seek to draw on the behaviours and attitudes of others. Similarly, Ainsworth (2002) draws on the work of Solomon Asch (1951) to describe how group norms tend to provide a strong stimulus for individual conformity to collective values. These are helpful, in explaining not just the collective attitudes that sustain a culture but also the loyalty and camaraderie that characterise the relations between individuals and other group members.

The work of Ronald Rufo (2016) also draws on psychological concepts to understand how police organisations impact on the wellbeing of their officers, not least through the process whereby individuals are transformed from civilians into police officers. This process is focused, in particular, on emphasising the differences between themselves and the civilians they will police. Recruits are made aware of the need to remain in control and to never show weakness and that their enemy is the public. Simultaneously, they are expected to always act with integrity. This list of attributes, suggests Rufo, provides a rather ambitious set of values for a human being and, while enabling officers to perform well in their job, may have a negative impact on their wellbeing and their relationships outside the work environment. Rufo also articulates clearly the interplay between psychological and sociological concepts in the process of 'making' police officers. He states:

> The social conflicts and pressures the rookie faces have multiple dimensions that involve the rookie's relationships with family and friends as well as relationships with other officers and the civilian clientele encountered in his work, The conflicts and pressures alter his social relationships with all these people, and in terms of his internal psychological life, they shape and influence his evolving sense of a professional or occupational self. (2016: 8–9)

These conflicts and pressures inevitably have the potential to cause stress and, as Ainsworth (2002) points out, can be seen as being caused by particular external situations or the internalised response of the individual officer to them. Traditionally, authors adopting a cultural lens through which to write about the stress of police work have focused on the potential of the occupation to create these negative responses and on the specific challenges of the job as the cause (see, for example, Smith and Gray, 1983). Furthermore, such accounts tend to highlight the propensity of the occupation to generate conflict or to subject its practitioners to stressful encounters, and it is these that are seen as the causal factors rather than acknowledging the potential role played by individual factors.

Ainsworth (2002) also draws on work by J.D. Sewell (1983) to illustrate some examples of situations that provoke the occupational stress experienced by officers. The research asked officers to rank particular occurrences as to the level of stress they associated with them, and found that, perhaps unsurprisingly, many of these involved instances that posed specific threat or harm to the officer. For example, two of the top three situations that officers identified as stressful were 'violent death of a partner in the line of duty' and 'taking a life or shooting someone in the line of duty' (Ainsworth, 2002: 120). Increasingly, however, it is possible to identify evidence that proposes a different, and competing, set of reasons for the existence of stress among police officers. Research, such as that conducted by Pamela Collins and A. Gibbs (2003), suggests that, in fact, 'organisational issues rather than operational events are most likely to lead to incidents of stress' (Cockcroft, 2013: 139). Indeed, many of the drivers of stress can be seen as located within the structure and culture of the police occupational world rather than solely in those situations that officers encounter while working the streets. As noted previously, while the work of Sewell (1983) stressed the importance of traumatic and violent events as a reason for some instances of police stress, some of the research's findings might be considered more surprising. For example, those officers who participated in the research reported that unsuccessfully applying for promotion was as stressful as the pursuit of an armed individual. Likewise, having to deal with rioters was viewed as considerably less stressful than being the subject of an internal investigation. Furthermore, involvement in a hostage situation was ranked as less stressful than witnessing corrupt police activity. The work of Derek Summerfield (2011), a clinician writing in the *British Medical Journal*, appears to support this. He suggests that many post-traumatic stress disorder diagnoses among police officers are driven not so much by individual situations experienced as part of their occupational role but through the ongoing challenges of working within the particular structural and cultural environments of police organisations. Indeed, the context of organisational disenchantment and interpersonal conflict appeared to be such common facets of the police world that some medical practitioners tended to invoke a 'wear and tear' model of police stress that, in some cases, saw long careers in the organisation as a legitimate claim for early retirement on grounds of ill health. Integral to Summerfield's analysis is the perception that police organisations fail to take appropriate interest in the mental health of those officers they employ.

Four key issues can therefore be seen as emerging from research into police stress. First, that not all stressful events (as perceived by officers) are caused by the more directly and explicitly dangerous elements of their job. The mundane tensions, conflicts and disappointments that characterise much of everyday organisational life play a considerable and substantial role in this process. Second, that it is often the cumulative impact of stressful factors rather than one-off and extraordinary circumstances that lead to many of the diagnoses of stress among officers. Third, while some accounts of police work portray the occupational culture of the police as having a palliative effect for officers (see, for example, Waddington, 1999), there is some evidence, outlined above, to suggest that elements of the culture might, in fact, have a reverse effect. Finally, it is seen that the structure and culture of police organisations may actively mitigate against the effective development of mechanisms to deal with stress.

The work of Rufo (2016) also addresses the concept of the 'sixth sense' that has been seen as a facet of the police working culture. This refers to the intuition whereby an officer feels that they can assess the truth of a situation even in the absence of substantive evidence. One example of this is to be found in my oral history of the Metropolitan Police between the 1930s and 1960s (Cockcroft, 2001), when a former detective recounted, 'I'm nothing special but I feel that I can instinctively know when a person's telling the truth, whether he's genuine or not' (2001: 190).

To Rufo (2016: 10), this process is one of 'synthesizing and deducing' experiences held in our unconscious. The challenge, however, lies in the fact that this 'sixth sense' is an unconscious process that takes place without recourse to conscious analytic thought processes. Where this presents challenges is the fact that police officers are viewed as having a negative world view (see Reiner, 2010, for a description of police pessimism/cynicism) that represents a distorted view of reality. In Rufo's work (2016), a retired police officer recounts an experiment he conducted with two very different classes he was teaching. The first was a class of young students undertaking undergraduate degrees in criminal justice with a view to entering a range of roles within the criminal justice system such as those of probation officer, prison officer and police officer. The second class was composed of experienced police officers who had returned to college to undertake an undergraduate degree, most of whom were motivated to do so for either personal reasons or so they could work towards promotion. Rufo asked each of the classes what they consciously thought of when he mentioned the phrase 'Boy Scout leader'. For those younger students, who had yet to take up a role within the criminal justice system, their views were almost all positive. Their responses drew attention to the positive aspects of working with children, their dedication and their sacrifice. When the second class were given the same task, the results were markedly different. Every police officer implied, in Rufo's words, that, '*all* Boy Scout leaders were sexual predators, pedophiles, and sexual deviates, who could never be trusted with anyone' (2016: 11; original emphasis).

Such negative world views may therefore be a combination of prejudices, peer group pressure and work-based experience, and remind us of the way stereotypes can detract from objective thought processes and replace them with biased perceptual shortcuts. For example, Ainsworth (2002) uses an experiment conducted by Ben Duncan (1976) to illustrate this through identifying how differently people perceive the actions committed by people of one's own race and those by people of a different race. He made two short films that showed two people interacting in an increasingly hostile way. As the argument developed, the 'aggressor' pushed the other actor, the 'victim'. In one version of the film, the 'aggressor' was played by a black actor and, in the other, a white actor. What is of interest is that, when white people viewed the two films, only 13% of them perceived the behaviour of the white aggressor as 'violent behaviour'. However, 70% perceived the same behaviour committed by the black aggressor in the same way. Ainsworth (2002) concludes that this suggests that judgements about people's behaviour might be strongly influenced by the social group of the individual who makes that judgement, and this provides us with some insight into the relationship between internalised views at the individual level and wider group norms.

To a reader new to the idea of police culture, there is a bewildering array of subjects to consider in this area, and a number of challenges exist in respect of these. First, the number of areas that fall under the term are very wide. Police cultural studies can focus on subjects as diverse as camaraderie, discretion, corruption, racism, leadership and stress or indeed, any area that relates to the informal norms and values that are reproduced among police officers in their workplace. Second, as has been outlined in this chapter, there is a wide variety of different approaches to explore these issues, and these ways of understanding police culture are very much connected to particular academic subjects or disciplines. Unsurprisingly, these will all have quite different ways of framing the subject area of police culture, of determining what areas are important and of deciding how best to research it. At the same time, we should acknowledge that much of the work we might draw on to understand police culture is not always undertaken with the explicit intention of helping us to understand this phenomenon. For example, the research of psychologists working in the subject area of individual prejudice might help us to understand some elements of police behaviour through applying it to this topic despite the police culture context not being their original area of focus. It is this kind of approach that underpins much of the broad and diverse collection of writing about police culture – an area where research specifically into particular areas of the cultural values of policing sits next to ideas taken from work which, while focused on areas of police work, does not necessarily adopt a cultural perspective.

Questions for further consideration

1. Consider the different academic disciplines that contribute to our knowledge of police culture. What are the strengths and limitations of each in respect of their ability to further our knowledge of this area?
2. Reflect on the different motivations for those who approach research from an ethnographic position and those who adhere to an evidence-based policing (EBP) agenda. What is each trying to achieve?

Further reading

Fassin, D. (2017) 'Ethnographying the police', in D. Fassin (ed) *Writing the World of Policing: The Difference Ethnography Makes*, Chicago, IL: University of Chicago Press, pp 1–20.

Sherman, L. (1998) *Evidence-Based Policing*, Ideas in American Policing Series, Washington, DC: Police Foundation.

van Maanen, J. (1978) 'On watching the watchers', in P. Manning and J. van Maanen (eds) *Policing: A View From the Street*, Santa Monica, CA: Goodyear, pp 309–49.

4

Police culture and operational policing

This chapter will focus on what the knowledge base in this area tells us about operational policing and the ways in which police culture has been seen to influence the quality and nature of interactions with different sections of society. It will draw explicitly on research in the area to explore the impact of culture on interactions with groups defined by their ethnicity, gender and social class. Finally, it will chart the ways in which academic views have changed over time to accommodate more nuanced views of police culture, police behaviour and the relationship between the two.

The concept of police culture is inescapably entwined with that of operational policing. This is largely because it is in the arena of operational policing that the police are most likely to interact with members of the public. This is not to say that police culture and the behaviours and values only impact on non-police officers (police racism and sexism are well documented as problems experienced by female and minority ethnic police officers). However, to many authors and commentators, the first step to exploring police culture is to look at how the manifestations associated with it impact on the experiences of members of the public. Furthermore, it is these issues (for example, racism and sexism) that motivated early work in the area of police culture to attempt to link the values and attitudes held by officers with the experiences of members of the public who interact with them.

For a starting point, we need to understand why police culture, its impact on police behaviour and the subsequent way it is received or understood by the public are important. To answer this inevitably draws attention to the unique role that the police play in society and inescapably, to the concept of legitimacy. The work of Tom Tyler (1990) provides an excellent introduction to the concept of legitimacy that can be applied to any institution, organisation or authority regardless of the role they play in society. To Tyler (1990), the acceptance of authority by members of the public goes beyond merely conforming to rules and laws because of the fear of the negative consequences they will face if they do not act in accordance with them. Rather, it is the case that people accept such authority when they consider it legitimate, and legitimacy is achieved when people believe that the procedures they are subjected to by an institution, organisation or authority are carried out fairly. Of interest here is that Tyler's work makes it clear that perceptions of legitimacy are very much determined by how people are treated during an interaction rather than what the outcome of that particular interaction is. A person who is stopped and searched, for example, and subjected to further police action as a result of that stop and search procedure, despite being inconvenienced by it, might still consider that they have been treated fairly if the officer who conducted the procedure was courteous, respectful and fair. Furthermore, people perceive that, if the treatment they receive at the hands of a figure of authority is poor (for example, judgemental, rude or disrespectful), then they will believe that to be the view which that organisation or institution has of them. Clearly, therefore, legitimacy is a central concern when seeking to understand how operational police work effects the lives of the public.

The work of Mike Maguire (2008) points towards a growing sense of a 'crisis in legitimacy' (2008: 444) in policing that dates back to the 1970s. To Maguire, many of these legitimacy issues were associated with the work of detective units that had, over time, developed problematic standard working practices. In particular, Maguire points to five main areas that have caused concerns. First is the perceived ineffectiveness of the police in bringing offenders to justice. This relates not just to high-profile cases but also to low-level crime (or 'volume crime'). Second is a growing awareness of miscarriages of justice, particularly in cases where innocent members of the public were arrested and charged by the police. Third is an increasing public perception of police misuse of power and corrupt practices committed by police officers. Fourth is what was seen as a growing tendency for those personal freedoms enjoyed by the public to be limited by invasive investigative procedures. Finally, Maguire (2008) highlights an emerging sense that police practices were unaccountable and failed to exercise an appropriate degree of transparency. Legitimacy is therefore an important factor accounting for several dimensions of the police relationship with the public. Furthermore, an acknowledgement of this crisis of legitimacy has informed a number of police initiatives and policy changes aimed at improving police practices.

Police culture has been central to many of these discussions that view policing as lacking legitimacy. In particular, police culture is used by some as a means of explaining many of the essentially negative elements of policing and police work that research has identified. In an article from 2015 I propose a number of reasons to help explain this association between police culture and poor police practice (Cockcroft, 2015). For example, the concept of police culture emerged in parallel to, and sometimes in combination with, critical social scientific analyses of police practices. While it is not the case that all research into police culture paints a negative picture of it, even the most conservative estimate would suggest that a large proportion does. Significantly, this increasing scrutiny of police work and the attitudes, values and behaviours of its practitioners emerged at the same time as an increasingly questioning attitude on the part of the public towards all forms of authority. In short, therefore, the publicising of inappropriate police practices during the second half of the 20th century coincided with a growing concern by citizens about the use (and misuse) of state power, and the development in academia of more critical branches of social scientific thinking about these issues. It is also important to contextualise the policing crisis in respect of what is termed the 'Golden Age' of policing, a concept used by many writers addressing the history of British policing, such as Philip Rawlings (2002) and Robert Reiner (2010). The Golden Age of British policing refers to a period in the history of the British police broadly spanning the first half of the 20th century to the 1970s, which was characterised by a popular view of the British police officer (or 'bobby') as fair, honest and oriented towards public service (as opposed to crime fighting). In the eyes of many, this imagery became synonymous with a popular fictional British police officer of the time (depicted in feature films and TV series) named George Dixon, more popularly known as Dixon of Dock Green (Emsley, 2008). Clive Emsley, the historian, suggests, however, that this Golden Age of policing, tied up with the imagery of Dixon, may have less relevance to the reality of policing than many might think. He writes, 'Honest, upright, cool, calm, and avuncular with the public, with young tearaways and with "villains" alike, Dixon was an ideal type. He fitted what *The Times*, in its review of the film, called an "indulgent tradition" of the English police officer' (2008: 87).

The notion of the 'indulgent tradition' suggests that public appreciation for the police during the Golden Age of policing should not be viewed as being grounded in any real objective assessment of the police's work. Furthermore, while the processes outlined above showed how the appetite for critical scrutiny of the police increased substantially during the latter part of the 20th century, the scope for criticism was substantially increased through our comparison to the very different form of police behaviours we had come to associate with the halcyon days of the Dixon era. As shall become obvious in the remainder of this chapter, the public perception of the Golden

Age version of policing is difficult and unhelpful to apply to modern societies that have changed immeasurably since the post-war years of the 1950s.

Police work, in particular those forms that demand interaction with the public, provides very real challenges in respect of the perception of legitimacy. Three particular dimensions can be used as a starting point in respect of charting the relationship between police culture, operational policing and legitimacy: race, gender and social class. These should not, by any means, be taken as an exhaustive list given that further issues such as religion, age and sexuality (to name but a small number) also constitute potentially challenging areas in respect of legitimate policing. That said, race and gender provide examples of subjects that have attracted a range of academic commentary and formal initiatives, whereas social class is an area which, in terms of both its relationship to police culture and formal police recognition, has received substantially less attention.

Race

In modern times, the policing of race has provided one of the largest specific challenges for the police in respect of maintaining legitimacy. It is of particular note here that this issue has come to be seen as essentially embedded or intractable. From a US perspective, the work of Jerome Skolnick has been especially helpful. His 2007 essay 'Racial profiling – Then and now' (cited in Dunham and Petersen, 2017) suggests that any understanding of police–minority ethnic relations in the US has to be contextualised against the social and historical backdrop of race relations. In particular, he notes, the police were traditionally seen as responsible for controlling African Americans (especially in the more segregated southern states of the US) through the use of formal and informal mechanisms that were not applied to white Americans. As a result, Skolnick suggested that, by the 1960s, the majority of police officers held a significant level of prejudice against minority ethnic groups with this, unsurprisingly, leading to relationships between police and minority groups becoming characterised by tension and mistrust. At times, this generally negative relationship spilled over into highly visible protests and calls for political reform as a result of some well publicised cases of police abuse.

Despite the fact that evidence of police racial bias has led to significant reform and change in policing, widely held concerns continue to exist. The shooting of a black teenager, Michael Brown, in August 2014 by a white police officer provided the catalyst for a critical and vocal re-engagement of the debate over police and race under the '#BlackLivesMatter' banner. This, according to Rashawn Ray et al (2017), gained extra impetus in respect of its focus on police violence and its calls for community solidarity and social activism through its social media platform. While it is beyond doubt that much of the focus is on the experiences of minority ethnic groups in North America, such policing issues and the responses they illicit from minority ethnic communities are also a feature of British policing. In fact, Mike Brogden et al (1998) suggest that there is a notable consistency in the British and US experience of police racism over time, highlighting the 'pervasive problem of racist attitudes, assumptions and talk' (1998: 127). Furthermore, debates over police–minority ethnic relations often appear to largely focus on issues of 'over-policing', an overt focus on minority ethnic groups in respect of the police's crime fighting function. However, it is also important to understand that concerns remain over the ways in which minority ethnic groups access the service roles of the police. In particular, it has been noted by some academics that members of minority ethnic groups may also be less likely to experience quality of service in respect of the non-law enforcement elements of the police role.

Ben Bowling et al (2008) provide a helpful overview of the concept of racial discrimination and policing within the UK context. Recent decades have seen a substantial transformation in the experiences of members of black and Asian communities, and this has meant that they are much more likely today to 'make a significant contribution to the social, economic and political life of British society' (2008: 611). However, racist beliefs and attitudes still permeate British society, and research suggests that these still lead to the emergence of unhelpful stereotypes about certain ethnic groups. In turn, these common stereotypes have been viewed as a consistent factor contributing to racist beliefs and attitudes on the part of police officers, and it is these prejudices that are perceived as leading to differential policing experiences between racial groups. One of the concepts that we can use to understand the ways in which the police develop prejudicial practice is through Skolnick's idea of the 'symbolic assailant' (1994: 44). The 'symbolic assailant' is linked to Skolnick's belief that police officers develop cognitive short cuts, based on visual and audible cues (such as appearance and speech), which allow officers to estimate the propensity an individual has to cause them harm. In this way, according to Skolnick, 'the police officer responds to the vague indication of danger suggested by appearance' (1994: 44). This process, however, is not particularly accurate in that it tends to very much over-identify harmful individuals, given that it is based on stereotypes, especially when used in specific locations. This, Skolnick acknowledges, is a particular issue in that it means that law-abiding members of communities may be engaged with by the police in ways they consider unsatisfactory.

One of the most well-known examples of the apparently racially prejudiced nature of some policing, in the UK, is the flawed investigation into the murder of Stephen Lawrence and the subsequent inquiry led by Lord Macpherson. Stephen Lawrence was a black teenager who was stabbed to death by a group of young white males in South London in 1993. According to Tim Newburn (2008), the police investigation into the killing was marred by 'professional incompetence' (2008: 97) that saw little attempt to seek the suspects, drew complaints about the unprofessional treatment by the police of Lawrence's family and identified weaknesses in police intelligence, surveillance and searches. A significant conclusion of Lord Macpherson's report was that, while in many ways these issues came about as a lack of professionalism on the police's part, a further significant issue, that of racism, had a part to play. In particular, notes Newburn (2008), the issue of black victimisation appeared to be a consistent factor in the low levels of professionalism displayed by officers dealing with the case. This was particularly evident in the way the police communicated with the Lawrence family and Stephen Lawrence's friend (and witness to the crime), Duwayne Brooks. These factors led Lord Macpherson to conclude that the police were 'institutionally racist', a claim that would have a very considerable impact on British policing over the coming years. Institutional racism, according to Macpherson, can be defined in the following way:

> The collective failure of an organisation to provide an appropriate and professional service to people because of their colour, culture, or ethnic origin. It can be seen or detected in processes, attitudes and behaviour which amount to discrimination through unwitting prejudice, ignorance, thoughtlessness and racist stereotyping which disadvantage minority ethnic people. (1999: 634)

The key significance of the labelling of the police service in this way was to introduce a wholly new means of conceptualising police racism. Previously, police racism, in the UK at least, was framed as an individual issue rather than an institutional one, with racist officers being portrayed as 'bad apples' (that is, racist individuals who acted inappropriately regardless of the cultural values of the institution). The adoption by Lord Macpherson of the notion of institutional racism to describe the police effectively shifted the responsibility for racism away from the individual and onto police organisations as a whole. This was in marked contrast to the findings of a previous government inquiry led by Lord Scarman, who had been tasked with exploring the causes of civil disturbances that occurred in towns and cities in the early 1980s. The most notable of these were the Brixton riots of April 1981, which had been precipitated by a heavy-handed Metropolitan Police operation called 'Operation Swamp 81' and that had used 'sus' laws to stop and question individuals. According to Ben Bowling and Coretta Phillips (2003), out of 943 people stopped under 'Operation Swamp 81', only 75 were charged, and it was this apparent over-policing that caused deep resentment among members of that area's minority ethnic population.

The apparently racialised focus of the police actions led to a public outcry and exacerbated existing tensions in other British cities, leading to further unrest and disorder. As police–minority ethnic relations increasingly took centre stage, pressure increased for the state to take action to explore the causes and to provide remedies to ensure such occurrences were avoided in the future. Lord Scarman was duly appointed to head an inquiry into the disturbances, which, in time, reported on the causes and forwarded recommendations such as to increase the proportion of minority ethnic groups within police forces. In contrast to Lord Macpherson's report, which was published over 15 years later, Lord Scarman (1982) had suggested that police racism was essentially a problem caused by individual officers rather than the values of police organisations as a whole, and therefore stopped short of branding the police institutionally racist. The difference in tone between the reports is of interest for a number of reasons.

First, it shows that, over a relatively short period of time, the official discourse used to explain tensions between the police and minority ethnic communities had changed dramatically. Second, the Macpherson report evidences the growing political will of the time to send out a robust message that the problematic relationship between the police and minority ethnic communities was, from now on, to be presented as a problem caused by the police per se rather than individual officers. Third, in placing the responsibility for poor experiences of police work by minority ethnic populations firmly with the police, the state was effectively sending a strong signal that the British police would be required to undergo a period of cultural change and transformation.

This last point is especially significant in terms of police occupational culture. The tension between the Scarman and Macpherson reports in terms of content provides a helpful means of understanding the differences between two main ways of accounting for police behaviour. Lord Scarman's report, in highlighting the importance of the individual officer, is essentially forwarding a 'bad apple' explanation that seeks to limit responsibility for police actions to the individual officer. This reduces the culpability of the police organisation, and the individual racist officer is seen in the same way as one would view any other 'deviant' (to use the word in a criminological rather than pejorative sense). Such individual accounts had been the traditional way in which police organisations shaped the discourse around poor police practice and allowed the police institution to distance itself from such behaviours in light of the appropriate practice engaged in by other officers. In many ways, this position broadly parallels one that criminologists might term 'individual positivism'. The 'bad apple' does not choose to engage in such behaviours, nor are they compelled to do so by the values and culture of the organisation. Quite simply, their individual make-up and orientation accounts for their behaviour. Positioning poor police behaviour in such a way is not unproblematic. Obviously, it is a quite simple approach and one that fails to engage with ideas that highlight the influence of occupational, group and other social dynamics. Approaches that highlight the impact of culture on police behaviour are more broadly aligned to a criminological position of sociological positivism, where the cultural pressures of the police role and organisation can shape police attitudes and behaviours in particular ways. However, this position is also open to challenge. While individual positivism focuses on individual factors and fails to reflect on the potential influence of the cultural factors of the police organisation, sociologically positivist approaches focus on the cultural elements that impact on the individual without really engaging with their ability to ignore culture and to determine their own orientation to their work.

Here, of course, we find ourselves engaging with a tension highlighted earlier in this book when discussing the contribution of psychology to our understanding of police culture. At times, it can feel that we are expected to believe that police behaviour is a result either of cultural factors or, alternatively, of personal psychology. Traditionally, literature in the area of police culture has not made it that easy to reconcile these two positions, although, as we will see in later chapters, the work of Janet Chan (1997) has made it easier to conceptualise police culture in a way that accounts for the inclusion of a degree of individual free will or agency. Similarly, this relationship between the occupational culture of the police and the individual psychological or cognitive make-up of individual police officers draws us inescapably to the challenge of understanding the ways in which individual officers 'engage with', or, alternatively, are 'influenced by', the culture. This book will, at a later stage, address the idea (proposed by Campeau, 2015) that police culture should be conceived more as a tool for officers to use when required, rather than an unavoidable set of influences that strongly determine officer behaviour. However, we should remain aware, at this point, that the general tone of much writing about police culture is that there is a considerably strong relationship between culturally informed values and the behaviours that police officers engage in.

This relationship is particularly pertinent to the issue of police racism and prejudice, as evidenced by the work of Janet Foster (1989), who asserted that there are two forms of police racism. One is when police officers hold racist beliefs and act on such prejudices, and the other is when such police officers do not act on these prejudices. This issue provides complex challenges for police organisations. To what extent should personally and privately held views that are prejudicial be a barrier to employment when that individual acts in a professional manner? To what extent are police notions of professionalism based on occupationally exhibited behaviour or privately held opinion? While it might be tempting to suggest that personally held racist opinions, in the post-Macpherson world, should be a barrier to employment for potential police officers, would this mean that we were similarly required to gauge aspiring officers' views on a whole host of issues (for example, gender, religion, sexuality and class) before allowing them to become police officers? Obviously, therefore, the greater part of this argument appears to be determined by the extent to which we can understand the relationship between people's attitudes and their behaviour. That is, do people act in accordance with personally held opinions and views, or do their behaviours instead reflect the professional obligations that their organisation expects of them?

One of the key difficulties facing us when we explore the relationship between race and the culture of policing is not just that that attitudes towards race and ethnicity have evolved over time in wider society, but that the police have increasingly positioned themselves as an institution that is sensitive to and inclusive of all ethnic groups within society. While the success of the initiatives associated with such principles might be subject to robust discussion, such changes do make it difficult to assess whether the traditionally viewed racial prejudice of the police is a central tenet of the cultural landscape or more subject to change and fluctuation as a result of other factors. For example, the publication of the Macpherson report was described as 'a pivotal moment in the history of the police and race relations' by Megan O'Neill and Simon Holdaway (2007: 254), and led to the acceptance by the government of 70 recommendations aimed at eradicating behaviours and practices that were deemed to be unfair or discriminatory, to enhance inspection regimes, to increase transparency to the public and to strengthen legislation (Bowling et al, 2008). Similarly, Bowling et al (2008) note how the recommendations made by Lord Macpherson led to an increased focus on stop and search powers, recruitment from minority ethnic groups, training, complaints and disciplinary procedures, first aid, and family, victim and witness liaison.

They go on to suggest, however, that a substantial challenge of the post-Macpherson era has been to assess the extent to which the recommendations have been acted on, and whether real and effective change has been realised. One of the key areas of contention here, they claim, is that many of the positive changes associated with the Macpherson report have been negatively impacted by other developments in policy and legislation. For example, the government's intention to end police discrimination has, arguably, been undermined by the implicit discrimination against members of the Muslim faith that is assumed to be contained within anti-terrorism legislation such as the Anti-Terrorism Act of 2001. Of further interest here, note Bowling et al (2008), is that the Macpherson report, and its recommendations, did divide opinion and provoked support and opposition among police and non-police audiences alike. In particular, the issue of 'institutional racism' led to some believing that it unfairly labelled all officers as racist, regardless of individual officers' professional orientation and behaviour. Similarly, by playing down individual culpability, it was viewed by some as an impediment to dealing with those particular officers who did engage in discriminatory language, behaviour and practices. Conversely, some rejected the recommendations made by Macpherson, believing that there were, in fact, no problems of racial discrimination within the police.

The post-Macpherson era of policing has emerged against a backdrop of profound social change. This has meant that it has been difficult to chart the real impact of Lord Macpherson's recommendations on the police. Despite this, the work of Bethan Loftus (2009) draws attention to how the 'new politics of policing diversity' (2009: 35) provide a counterpoint to the traditional cultural position of the police. In doing so, the rise in 'identity politics' has led to the embedding of expectations within policing of equality in respect of a range of characteristics including ethnicity, gender and sexuality. The impact of this, claims Loftus, is twofold. First, it has changed the way in which police officers express views that might be consistent with their cultural beliefs (if these are racially discriminatory). Second, it has substantial implications for how police officers interact, and communicate, with members of different ethnic groups. One of the problems with this development is that 'The language of diversity comes to be seen as a tokenistic and politically correct gesture that, whilst impacting on how officers express themselves, does little if anything to alter their opinions and values' (Cockcroft, 2013: 103). This subsequently raises substantial issues regarding the impact of Lord Macpherson's recommendations on police officers at the individual level. Recent research also highlights newly identified dynamics in the relationship between policing and race. For example, the work of Lisa Long and Remi Joseph-Salisbury (2019) shows how black mixed-race men, due to visual cues of black origin, expect to experience racial discrimination in their interactions with police officers. These findings are obviously disconcerting given the work undertaken by police organisations to encourage inclusive policing in the light of Lord Macpherson's observations. Furthermore, this in itself holds implications for the experiences of officers who may come from minority ethnic backgrounds. If Lord Macpherson's recommendations have failed to change attitudes, values and behaviours, then police institutions will continue to struggle to engage positively with diversity both within and outside the organisation.

Gender

Police culture has long been viewed as fundamentally gendered, having at its core predominantly masculine values (Young, 1991; Maguire and Norris, 1994; Skolnick, 1994; Reiner, 2010). The label of masculinity refers to many of the characteristics we might associate with sexism, but also incorporates wider features that pertain less to the direct denigration of females and more to the overtly male nature of police work and police organisations. Research into police culture has customarily focused on the essentially gendered nature of police work and highlighted those elements of police behaviour that are seen as rooted in a traditionally masculine world view such as sexism, violence and excessive drinking.

Similarly, Jennifer Brown (2007) begins her exploration of the importance of masculinity to policing by noting that it is perhaps one of the central themes in the occupational culture, and one that impacts on both the men and women who work in the organisation. Men find themselves in an environment where their status is commensurate to explicit displays of physicality and sexuality, and women find themselves sexually harassed and discriminated against on the grounds of their gender. While Brown notes that a number of changes have occurred over recent years that might be viewed as presenting a significant threat to the continued masculinity of the police organisation, such as those to the operational, managerial and legislative contexts of policing, these have not changed the fundamental orientation of the organisation. Women, she notes, are still judged 'in terms of what they are not rather than of what they are' (Brown, 2007: 223). In a similar vein, Marisa Silvestri (2003) draws attention to the inherently contradictory nature of the female police officer from the perspective of the police culture, noting that 'police work is defined culturally as an activity only "masculine men" can accomplish' (2003: 31).

The culturally enabled gender divide mirrors the traditional separation of male and female police officer roles that characterise much of the historical organisation of police work. In 1991, the crime and policing historian Clive Emsley described how the Metropolitan Police employed female staff to deal with females in custody as far back as the late 1800s. Similarly, during the same period, the Metropolitan Police developed the role of police matron (Cockcroft, 2013). The term 'matron' strongly describes the nature of the role that largely encompassed undertaking body searches of female offenders, and having responsibility for their general welfare. By the time of the First World War, the idea of female police volunteers was becoming increasingly widespread. This is evidenced by the fact that a Women's Police Service and Voluntary Women Patrols had been introduced by this time, although it must be said that these roles focused very much on the welfare, as opposed to the crime fighting, role of the police, and were largely limited to the moral protection of vulnerable females. It is also of interest to note here that the Police Federation, the staff association of police officers serving at below the rank of superintendent, was opposed to the introduction of female police officers until 1947 (see Cockcroft, 2013). Even the Sex Discrimination Act of 1975, which effectively sought to remove inequalities in the workplace, did not lead, according to Silvestri (2003: 47), to complete 'gender-integration' in the police.

This separation of roles has continued to be reflected in police organisations throughout recent history, although since 1995, with the appointment of Pauline Claire as Chief Constable of Lancashire, female officers have become appointed to senior leadership positions on a fairly regular basis. However, Silvestri (2017) warns us that this should not be taken as evidence that gender inequality is no longer an issue to be tackled. Instead, she suggests that, while the appearance of equality has been achieved, the reality, sadly, has not. In particular, echoing the findings of Brown (2007) a decade earlier, she concludes that gender neutrality has not fully permeated the structure and culture of the organisation.

The gender divisions that policing has traditionally been viewed as being built on have wider impacts beyond issues such as career progression. One area of particular interest here is that police cultures may impact on the ways in which the female public experience interaction with the police. Research suggests that sexist values, connected to the culture, may cause female victims of gendered crime (for example, sexual assault, rape and harassment) to experience a poor-quality or inappropriate service from male police officers. According to Louise Westmarland (2001), male officers generally find dealing with female victims of gendered crime difficult. As a result, in a later piece of work Westmarland (2017) goes on to suggest that the male-based views that inform police work make female officers the obvious choice to deal with the more gendered elements of the role, such as work with children and female victims. After all, she states, 'Women "instinctively" know about children and will be "naturally" more sympathetic when dealing with victims of sexual assault because they "know how it feels"' (2017: 303). By the same token, male officers often appear reluctant to engage with female offenders. Research conducted in Scotland by Suzanne Young (2015) found that male officers often held negative views of female offenders, viewing them as hostile, manipulative and uncooperative. As a result, male officers often felt very uncomfortable and lacking in confidence when dealing with cases in which they had to arrest females. Such subtleties of the relationship between gender and policing can be viewed as a direct consequence of the stereotyping about the female gender, facilitated by the essentially masculine values that inform the culture of the police. These stereotypes arise as a result of the very simplistic assumptions that have been seen, traditionally, as being integral to police views on gender. Accordingly, police views of females are often seen as operating around simplistic dichotomies such as 'wife/whore' (Heidensohn, 1985) or 'rough/respectable' (Cain, 1973; see also Cockcroft, 2013). The obvious problems we can foresee here are that these frameworks of understanding are incredibly unhelpful as a means of enabling male police officers to appropriately relate to females across the spectrum of potential situations through which they might interact with them.

One female officer, quoted in Ian Loader and Aogán Mulcahy (2003: 215), articulates the limitations of such culturally informed ways of understanding gender when she stated, 'When I joined you were either a nymphomaniac or a dyke, you couldn't be normal'.

As noted above, these simplistic views of gender can be seen to impact police responses to gendered crimes. For example, historical work (such as that of Brogden, 1991) notes how police intervention in domestic matrimonial issues (such as domestic violence) was, for much of the 20th century, opposed not just by the culture of the police but also by the formal structure of the police, with those officers who did intervene putting themselves at risk of being formally disciplined. In part, such responses to gendered crime reflect the attitude, which prevailed for much of the 20th century, that the criminal law was something to be applied to people's public, rather than private, behaviour. This is articulated by the Wolfenden Committee (1957), which, reporting on the purpose of criminal law, noted that it was there:

> ... to preserve public order and decency, to protect the citizen from what is injurious and to provide sufficient safeguards against exploitation or corruption of others.... It is not ... the function of the law to intervene in the private lives of citizens ... further than is necessary to carry out [these] purposes. (Wolfenden, 1957, cited in Jefferson, 2009: 9)

This, it can be argued, gave impetus to a style of policing that saw it as beyond the scope of the law to intervene in the domestic lives of adults taking place behind closed doors. The complexities of the gendered culture of policing become even more pronounced when one explores the relationships that emerged between police officers and prostitutes, an area explored through oral histories of policing (see Brogden, 1991; Weinberger, 1995; Cockcroft, 2001). This particular relationship is of interest as prostitution was an occupation that muddied the symmetry of the culture's assumptions surrounding gender. Its practitioners were (according to the aforementioned works, at least) generally female. The act of prostitution itself, while not illegal, was in many respects criminalised through the application of laws against those activities that supported it. While the degree of illegality involved in prostitution might be somewhat ambiguous, the act was considered, in respect of the predominant values of society, as morally deviant. From the outset, therefore, we can identify an emerging tension as prostitutes operated within a legal context that was largely legislated against, which attracted the moral censure of wider society and yet, as a group, were characterised by a substantial degree of vulnerability. Such factors, taken together, challenge the rigid gender classifications described above. Further complications came, however, from the fact that there appeared to be an implicit empathy between the roles of police officer and prostitute, in large part due to the vulnerability of both positions, the unsociable hours and the fact that the natural terrain of both practitioners was the urban street. This can be seen in extracts from my oral history of policing between the 1930s and 1960s:

> We had a good working relationship with the girls.... I always fully endorse that there was a great deal of camaraderie between the girls and uniform ... they weren't too keen on the OPD Squad ... that's Outrage and Public Decency.... (Cockcroft, 2001: 148)

> ... It's a funny thing ... but I met a tom [police slang for prostitute] ... a few years ago now ... and she said, "We were a little community weren't we?" I said, "Well, yes ... in a strange way that's true" ... the night duty coppers would get up about the same time as the night duty denizens ... (Cockcroft, 2001: 149)

> ... I remember there was one prostitute ... [name removed] ... and she was never arrested ... never ... and this was because she had once helped save a copper when he was taking a beating off some blokes.... (Cockcroft, 2001: 148)

Part of the value of these extracts is that it allows us to explore, critically, some of the more deterministic ways in which gender is seen to be constructed within the culture of the police. What becomes apparent is that the nuanced and excluded status of the prostitute certainly appeared to be accorded some respect by police officers. Likewise, it is difficult to detect a sense of the 'wife/whore' or 'rough/respectable' distinctions proposed by Frances Heidensohn (1985) and Maureen Cain (1973). More accurately, perhaps, if such distinctions did exist it appeared to make little difference to how police officers interacted with prostitutes or formed their opinions of them. In turn, this serves to remind us of the challenging nature of understanding the gendered nature of police work. Undoubtedly, however, the masculinity that shapes the values of the police organisation continues to influence the experiences of females, both as police officers and as members of the public. Furthermore, while some of the more obvious gendered barriers have provoked positive reforms in recent years, other gendered differences are still being identified. Female recruitment to the police remains relatively strong, with 29% of all officers, in England and Wales in 2017, being female (House of Commons Library, 2018). However, US-based research by Diane Elliot et al (2015) points to female police officers being more likely to experience burn-out than their male colleagues, with the authors identifying lack of mentoring and integration, sexual harassment and the impact of home life as significant factors. Importantly, their research, especially with reference to the latter point, provides us with a reminder of the continued gender divisions that exist, not just in the workplace but also in the domestic sphere.

Social class

The policing of social class is integral to our understanding of policing and the culture that has grown around it. To start with, our understanding of police history is bound by dissenting ideological perspectives which, to a large degree, present very different ideas surrounding the extent to which the key driver or rationale behind the introduction of the 'new' police in 1829 was the control of the working classes. Robert Reiner (2010) does much to highlight our contested understanding of the history of British policing, and shows how these two ideologically driven accounts, the Orthodox and the Revisionist, largely mirror wider contemporary political divisions. The Orthodox account suggests that the police were introduced as a rational response to problems of crime and disorder that emerged from the unprecedented population growth that accompanied the Industrial Revolution. In his exploration of this period, Philip Rawlings (2002) showed how the social changes of the time demanded a formalised response, not least in respect of the issue of maintaining order. The first of these changes was the growth in population. In the period between 1550 and 1820, notes Tony Wrigley (1990), the population of England increased by 280%, leading to London growing from quite a modest size to being the largest city in Europe. This shift caused a decline in wages and an increase in prices. In turn, this led to a greater degree of geographical mobility among the workforce that inflamed wider concerns regarding the potential threat to order posed by the working classes. Prior to this time, Rawlings (2002) notes, the law quite simply had little impact on the lives of most working people, who generally policed themselves via informal means. Where control was needed, it was often found through institutions such as charity schools, workhouses and houses of correction, rooted in a system that paid broadly similar amounts of respect to the concepts of punishment and welfare. Under such a system, a formal bureaucratic police function was simply not required. However, a number of factors converged to create what Rawlings (2002) identifies as the 'Crime Panic of 1848'. The reasons for this increase in crime were diverse and ranged from the spread of new labour practices (which led to some social unrest), the growth of new urban areas and the expansion of cities (as workers left rural areas to find work in larger conurbations) and the return of servicemen from overseas service. Rawlings also recognises social class as a persistent theme in the history of British policing, and shows how concerns about the behaviour of the poor had a long history of being translated into legislation with which to control them. On this point, Rawlings is unequivocal: 'To say that many of these laws were aimed at working-class people is uncontroversial since this was their purpose: the behaviour of the rich might be regarded as scandalous, rarely as criminal' (2002: 155).

Furthermore, he continues by stating that:

> The poor were also hemmed in by laws on morality which worked to constrain their lives. Crime, illegitimacy, idleness, irreligion, poaching, drinking, dancing, the playing of games and so forth were believed to be linked. These activities were, therefore, criminalized, as were the places, such as alehouses, in which the poor engaged in them. (Rawlings, 2002: 51)

This sense of concern over the morality and behaviour of the poor was exacerbated by the movement of the working classes from the perceived tranquillity of rural villages to the altogether more dynamic (and some might say chaotic) environments of newly industrialised towns and cities. This is illustrated through the work of Shebbear (1776), who noted that 'in London amongst the lower classes all is anarchy, drunkenness and thievery – in the country good order, sobriety and honesty' (cited in Rawlings, 2002: 62). To authors whose work can be characterised as conforming to the Orthodox approach, the specific impact of class does not feature as part of the reason why the new police were introduced. However, to the ideological opponents of the Orthodox approach, the Revisionists, class was integral to their introduction. According to Reiner (2010), the Revisionists saw the rapid expansion of industrialised towns and cities as leading to greater segregation between social classes. As the poorer, more working-class areas of these environments became more prone to criminal activity, so the wealthier areas demanded greater protection. At the same time, there emerged a growing consensus that riot and disorder among the working class (their traditional means of expressing discontent) was no longer seen as something to be tolerated but as a legitimate threat to order. Similarly, the advent of industrialisation changed the nature of social relations through a need to wield even greater control over the working classes. The result was that the police officer was cast (in the words of Storch, 1976) as a 'domestic missionary' and tasked with controlling the lower classes in ways that would make them more able to meet the demands of the new ways of working that had emerged as a result of the Industrial Revolution. As is evident from the above discussion, our historical understanding of the introduction of the police is subject to some controversy, and this tension is situated firmly around the extent to which policing focuses on social class rather than the policing of crime.

Such discussions have provided a critical undercurrent to discussions about policing, police behaviour and police culture over many years. In particular, since the 1970s, when the Revisionist viewpoint was established, there has been a specific academic focus on the concept of class, although such concerns have not (unlike in respect of race and gender) generated particular attention within the police institution. Indeed, Brogden et al (1988: 145) concluded their analysis of the issue of class discrimination by suggesting that 'It really is not a very radical thing to say in 1987 that the system of criminal justice, and that obviously includes policework, is class based'. This issue of class also collides with other categories of identity that raise issues for police culture, like that of race. Implicit here, as Brogden et al (1988) note, is that most of the minority ethnic males stopped by the police will be members of the working classes. Class, therefore, generates differential impacts throughout the criminal justice system. Howard Becker (1963, cited by Brogden et al, 1988) illustrates this by stating that middle-class males, when apprehended by the police, are less likely than working-class males to be taken by police officers to a police station. If they are taken to a police station they are less likely to have their behaviour formerly recorded. Subsequently, middle-class males are less likely than their working-class counterparts to be convicted or sentenced as a result of their behaviour. Class, therefore, to many authors, provides the founding social division in policing on which others are constructed and this, in turn, reflects the Revisionist interpretation of policing. Brogden et al reiterate this when they note that 'Radical researchers on policework of course have all argued that the most important form of police discrimination is that based on social class. Race, sex and age factors may compound this original discrimination, but the class structure, in line with classical Marxist theory, is the paramount one' (1988: 142).

A further dynamic lies in the fact that the police, according to Brogden et al (1988), are acutely aware of the ways in which different social groups can cause different forms of resistance to the police, and that this therefore contributes to the differential approach to class. Simply put, the working classes are viewed as a potential physical threat to the police but less capable of causing more substantial problems. This draws us to what Robert Skidelsky (1975) terms the 'pro-police' mentality of the police, which prioritises self-preservation in the face of potential attacks on police credibility. This is supported by the following extract taken from my oral history of London policing that presents an officer's views of policing clashes between supporters of the British Union of Fascists and opposing left-wing groups during the 1930s:

> ... You wouldn't feel very friendly disposed to either of them and, on the other hand, the communists ... a lot of them ... were fairly well-educated people and, so, you were always warned ... if you had a decent Inspector in charge ... was if you were going to take any action make sure that your action is justified ... that it can be justified. What do you do? Because they're not fools, the majority of them, they weren't fools. They were quite an educated people and so ... if you took any really excessive action ... you were in trouble.... (Cockcroft, 2001: 182)

Other oral histories, however, provide some support for a more traditional view of the way that policing positioned itself in respect of class, by presenting a more straightforward account of the police that sees their only opposition as coming from the lower end of the socio-economic structure. For example, the work of J. White (1983) drew on the oral testimony of working-class members of the public and concluded that the role of the police was one of 'sworn custodians of ... class justice' (1983: 39). That said, one of the peculiarities of the class dynamic of the police–public relations is that the police themselves have traditionally been drawn from the same demographic sector of the population as the people they police. This has led some commentators (see, for example, Brogden, 1991) to draw attention to the relevance of the fact that policing itself was a working-class occupation and one whose members were as marginalised by the police institution in respect of their class as those they policed.

Changing contexts

If one looks to the work of Bethan Loftus, there is another explanation as to why the concept of social class should concern us, especially in respect of how we understand police culture. While social class is often presented in terms akin to other characteristics such as race and gender, arguably it needs to be understood in a fundamentally different way. The reason is quite straightforward. While race and gender have created incredibly important (and often very difficult) dynamics for the police in respect to how they effectively and appropriately interact with individuals, the discourse around such subjects has changed. While it would be wrong, and also very inaccurate, to suggest that discrimination along lines of race and gender has been eradicated, it is fair to say that the context and politics of such issues have changed. Taking the issue of race, in a UK context, much of the argument about the social role, effectiveness and fairness of policing has centred on landmark events such as the Brixton riots of 1981 (and its aftermath), the murder of Stephen Lawrence and subsequent publications such as the Scarman and Macpherson reports. These have changed the way in which the police address the race issue, the language that is used and the expected standards shown by police officers towards members of minority ethnic groups. Likewise, the gendered nature of policing has, arguably, over the last two decades been increasingly addressed by police organisations. Again, in the UK context, there are cases such as that of Alison Halford, an Assistant Chief Constable in the Merseyside Police, whose repeated failure to be promoted led to her bringing a claim that eventually resulted in settlement between the two parties and to a growing acknowledgement of the career progression challenges faced by female officers. Similarly, as Heidensohn (2008) shows, gendered crimes such as domestic violence and sexual abuse have become an increasingly important focus for the police after having been neglected for much of the past. As a result, the needs of female victims of crime are met with a substantially greater degree of sympathy (by both police officers and organisations) and, accordingly, new resources, procedures and expectations.

Despite the progress made towards gender equality in policing over recent years, Silvestri (2015) strikes a note of caution. The impact of reduced police budgets and moves towards cutting bureaucracy within the public sector do potentially mean that initiatives aimed at challenging inequality may be under threat. Similarly, she notes that mechanisms of female equality such as the Government Equalities Office and the Equalities and Human Rights Commission have recently witnessed a ratcheting down of their scope and resources. Furthermore, the advent of Police and Crime Commissioners has, she claims, done little to shape a collective agenda aimed at promoting equality.

While the debate will always continue as to whether or not the changes that have been made to provide a greater level of service to females and members of minority ethnic groups have actually had a beneficial impact, the issue of social class remains relatively unaddressed by academics. This may well be because class is increasingly a rather intangible concept to measure or identify. However, the sociologist Jock Young (2007) dispels the idea that class is no longer a relevant or valid concept. Instead, he draws attention to the ways in which its impact has changed. Previously, and for much of the 20th century, social class operated at a structural level where an individual's social class was easy to identify through their occupation, their income and where they lived. Nowadays, the concept is more fluid and operates at an altogether more cultural level, where such identifications are made not so much on factual information but based on more visible cues such as fashion, speech and behaviour. Furthermore, evidence suggests that class continues to be an important social category drawn on by police officers. This may, in part, be because of the work that has been undertaken over recent years to rectify police weaknesses in respect of their treatment of females and members of minority ethnic communities. The work of Bethan Loftus (2009) and Chris Haylett (2001, cited in Loftus, 2009) highlights the ways in which social class has arguably become the key criteria when identifying groups which represent an appropriate focus for discretionary police attention (see Cockcroft, 2013). In this way, notes Loftus (2009: 45), 'poor, young, white men stand forward as the embodiment of disorder and distaste'.

Indeed, the ongoing impact of the Macpherson report, coupled with a growing appreciation of the experiences of gender within police organisations, has done much to counter explicitly racist and sexist attitudes. Police organisations have become increasingly diverse in two key respects. The first is in the broad range of people who are now recruited as officers in respect of personal characteristics such as gender, race, sexuality and level of education. The second relates to the formal acknowledgement of changes to police responses to particular groups and crimes. One example is the adoption of more robust approaches and policies pertaining to the policing of domestic violence. It is hoped that a stronger focus towards dealing with this form of crime effectively will lead to greater awareness of gendered crime at a cultural level among officers. There is still much to be done, however, in this regard, and the HMIC, in a report aimed at heightening awareness of domestic abuse, noted:

> From our inspection fieldwork, listening to victims of domestic abuse, surveying those working with those victims and from our engagement with practitioners, campaigners, academics, support networks and other service providers, the message is clear. There is insufficient awareness and understanding of domestic abuse by the police and the attitudes of some police officers are unacceptable. Attitudes and cultural issues need to be challenged properly and addressed by force leaders and supervisors, and officers need to be better equipped with the right skills and knowledge. (2014: 122)

It would be inaccurate and unhelpful to suggest that discriminatory attitudes and behaviours had been eradicated from policing. However, it is possible to suggest that inappropriate behaviour towards females and members of minority ethnic groups is less prevalent, or less overt, than was previously the case. And while sexist and racist attitudes might remain, there is less chance of these being overtly expressed given the 'new politics of policing diversity' (Loftus, 2009: 35) that have emerged within recent years, although there is a debate regarding the extent to which such values might merely have been pushed underground (see Cockcroft, 2013). Given the great attempts made by police organisations to tackle racism and sexism, the issue of social class remains largely under the radar. Reasons for this may include what Revisionists might see as the essentially, and traditionally, class-based nature of policing. However, the biggest reason that class remains one of the key characteristics by which the police can legitimately distinguish (or at least without fear of recourse) is the fact that gender and race have become protected characteristics whereby decisions in a workplace made on such characteristics are subject to legal action on the grounds of discrimination. Without such protected status, Loftus (2009: 160) suggests that the white male becomes 'unproblematic terrain' and attracts the type of discriminatory targeting that had previously been determined by an individual's ethnicity. In some respects, therefore, it can be seen that the white working-class male remains a 'target' for police attention.

Operational policing and cultural determinism

We have seen how the idea of police culture can impact at an operational level. The predominant, and traditional, view of police culture is that it represents a set of palpable values based, according to Edgar Schein (2004), on a set of underlying assumptions about the way the world works and normative ideas about the way the world should be. These, in turn, are viewed as a fundamental reason explaining the nature of police officer interaction with members of the public. Crucially, here, these values and assumptions are seen as leading (again drawing on Schein, 2004) to police officers modifying their behaviour on the basis of the personal characteristics of the individual or individuals with whom they are interacting. Female members of the public, as we have seen, are characterised on the basis of their gender and treated accordingly. In the same way, race is viewed as a factor that sometimes eclipses behaviour in determining the likely outcome of an encounter with the police.

This has been the traditional way in which police culture has been depicted. This approach has been undoubtedly helpful in allowing us to explain many of the characteristics of police–public interaction. In particular, it has facilitated our explanations of the experiences that different groups have in terms of their dealings with the police and, in doing so, it has allowed police organisations to identify discrepancies in service delivery and to put in place programmes of reform with which to improve practices.

However, from the late 1990s onwards, academics have begun to identify variations in police behaviour that appear to undermine the deterministic characteristics of the traditional police culture model. In particular, the idea that police organisations have a coherent and predictable culture that impacts on officer behaviour has been harder to defend in the light of research undertaken over recent years. Perhaps the most widely cited piece of research in this regard is that undertaken by Janet Chan (1997). Chan found that these traditional ways of understanding police culture were increasingly difficult to apply to modern policing. Significantly, her work suggested that culture was essentially a fluid concept. That is to say, it differs from the somewhat 'monolithic' (see Reiner 2010: 132) nature with which it is sometimes described. Older work appears to view police culture in a rather more simple way that is both linear and deterministic – linear in that it is predictable as a process of socialisation and deterministic in that it is equally predictable in its impact on the values and behaviours of police officers. Chan's work, however, signalled the beginning of a much more complex way of understanding police culture, not just in terms of its effects but also in terms of its causes. From Chan's work onwards, police scholars have begun to chart the complexities of police culture, the variety of forms it takes and, importantly, the array of factors that shape its various forms.

Simultaneous to advances in our understanding of police culture, not least in our appreciation of its scope, we have also begun to acknowledge another complicating factor. Since 2000 we have seen not only a rewriting of our understanding of police culture but also a series of changes and developments that will have impacted on police practice and, subsequently, on the ways in which police officers see their work. While such changes, for example in respect of race and gender, have been addressed above, it is interesting to see how contemporary police scholars see such changes to the police role and how they impact on the cultural orientation of the police. The recent research of Sarah Charman (2017) provides a fascinating insight into the ways in which police officers are socialised into their occupational identity and, conversely, what the role of 'police officer' means to them. Her work is important in that it identifies a substantial cultural shift away from the more established cultural values of crime fighting. Instead, today's police officers are more likely to have very different perceptions about what the police role is and what skills it requires. Increasingly, the new police officers that Charman studied were very much attuned to the 'welfare' or 'service' elements of the police role, rather than focusing solely on law enforcement. In doing so, they saw themselves as essentially different in outlook to the older officers with whom they worked and who avoided those elements of the role that had a more explicit service or welfare component. As a result, Charman was able to identify a new cultural orientation, among recently recruited officers, which resisted the traditional view of the welfare and service elements of the police role as essentially gendered work to be undertaken by female police officers. Instead, those elements of the police role that highlight safeguarding and the support of vulnerable populations were becoming increasingly seen as core police tasks.

Other variations in police culture have also been identified over recent years. For example, Jan Terpstra's (2017) work into the cultural differences between police officers working in urban and rural environments in the Netherlands shows how traditional ideas of police culture tend to be much more important to city-based police officers.

Officers based in more rural environments have a substantially different occupational role. Furthermore, the fact that officers in rural areas have a much larger geographical distance to cover leads to challenges in terms of operational back-up and support. This, Terpstra argues, leads to very different ideas among officers. For example, rural officers put considerable emphasis on the need for communication skills and the building of effective relationships with civilians. Of note, here, is that the difference between the two sets of officers is not the increased level of criminality and disorder in the urban setting but rather the higher level of 'craftmanship' (Terpstra, 2017: 27) displayed by the rural officers. For example, the depictions of urban policing described by the rural officers typified urban police officers as 'cowboys' (Terpstra, 2017: 27) and as lacking in skill. Similar research, undertaken in different countries, has also supported these findings, suggesting that such differences can be seen as relatively consistent regardless of national jurisdiction.

Increasingly, therefore, our understanding of police culture has moved away from the linear and deterministic representations of the past. Scholars of police culture have often referred to the ways in which police culture encourages inflexible and rigid thinking (for example, in the form of racial stereotyping and 'symbolic assailants') among police officers, and David Sklansky (2007) reminds us of the ways in which academics addressing the concept of police culture have also tended to be quite rigid in their approach to the subject. In doing so, he refers to the concept of 'cognitive burn-in' (2007: 20), whereby academic ideas and assumptions about police culture become embedded and unquestioned. This has become more important over time as quite dated ways of thinking about police culture have become accepted by some as having contemporary relevance. To recap, these assumptions and expectations can be summarised as follows: 'that police officers think alike; that they are paranoid, insular, and intolerant; that they intransigently oppose change; that they must be rigidly controlled from the outside, or at least from the top' (Sklansky, 2007: 20).

Hopefully, this chapter has shown that this is not necessarily true. As the work of Loftus (2010) highlights, contemporary policing has changed greatly since academics first started writing about police culture due to the growing diversity of police organisations, changes to the way they are structured and run and, of course, the growth of community policing. These changes have taken place against a rapidly changing society, leading to what Loftus refers to as the 'new social field of policing' (2009: 21). As a result, 'The era of simplistic binary depictions of police culture has given way to reference to the fluidity of police cultures' (Cockcroft, 2013: 103) and increasingly, police culture scholars are focusing not so much on the uniformity of police values and behaviours but on their scope for variation and change. Despite this, we need to be a little cautious about automatically discounting any sense of continuity, over time, in the reference points that act as symbolic anchors for police culture. Some elements of the culture, according to Loftus (2009), have remained very stable throughout its history, whereas others appear to feature less prominently across different eras and locations. To Eugene Paoline (2003) it is this relationship between the monolithic (that is, unchanging) and fluid (that is, changeable) nature of police culture that should provide the impetus for future research into police culture. Furthermore, he suggests that cultural differentiation, where we see a variety of forms of police culture, does provide a foundation from where we can simultaneously employ both monolithic and fluid models of police culture to understand the world of the police officer.

As Paoline (2003) indicates, there has been a substantial change in the way we portray police culture over a short period of time, with ideas being characterised at first as rigid and deterministic and more recently, as fluid and changeable (but with a certain degree of stability). To make sense of this, we really have to address the way in which police culture influences police officers' working lives. Police culture has often been viewed in a way that sees a straightforward relationship between values and action. That is to say, police officers are viewed as taking on board a certain set of values (derived from the occupational culture) through interaction with their peers and these, unproblematically, are viewed as directing the behaviour of police officers. One of the challenges with this approach is that it promotes an idea of police officers as being undiscriminating consumers of what the culture 'tells' them to do. As the work of Chan (1997) shows us, this is very problematic in that it creates a model of police culture that is deterministic, and one where all officers unthinkingly act in a way that accords with the underlying assumptions of the culture. This obviously overplays the role of culture while underplaying the scope of individual officers to navigate the culture on their own terms.

The work of Holly Campeau (2015) goes some way towards challenging this view of how police culture influences police values and action. An interesting part of the background to her work was that her research took place during a period in which the police organisation that she was studying was undergoing substantial change in the form of enhanced oversight of police practice. At such times, she claims, cultural knowledge is drawn on more consciously by officers, and this provides the perfect foundation from which to study the relationship between culture and action. In particular, she critiques the way in which police culture theorists have explored police culture by focusing on a specific set of values that are associated with the occupational culture. Police officers, in Campeau's theory, do not simply hold a set of inter-connected beliefs about the way the world is or should be. Therefore, she suggests that there is no police 'way of life' (2015: 672), in part because police officers have to act in ways that do not resonate with the attitudes that they hold. Instead, she proposes that police culture, rather than offering a set of values to internalise, presents to officers a set of resources (or a 'toolkit', 2015: 672), which they can then draw on when required to resolve a situation they face. Apart from providing a means of understanding police culture that parallels the way in which we understand culture in other areas of social life, this approach or model provides some real benefits for our understanding of policing. Campeau explains that studies of police culture usually identify data that supports the presence of factors such as sexism or camaraderie. However, where they are less successful is in finding consistency of police behaviour across groups of individual officers or among officers working in very different roles. By viewing culture as a set of resources rather than as a set of embedded values, we allow ourselves to understand why some police officers in particular situations will draw on cultural knowledge while others will not. Integral to this account, therefore, is the idea that police officers actively determine how and why to draw on cultural meaning as a resource, and that this, significantly, is determined by the characteristics of the situation in which they find themselves. Campeau's work therefore allows us to position police culture in a way that helps us to overcome many of the weaknesses that have become evident in academic accounts over recent years. One such example pertains to Sklansky's notion of 'cognitive burn-in' (2007: 20). The shift from understanding police culture as a set of values and reclassifying them as a resource will hopefully present a substantial shift in the way that academics position themselves to understand police culture, and how it is used by police officers in their day-to-day working lives.

Loftus's work provides an acknowledgement of the present state of police cultural studies. Her work suggests that police culture, and the way we conceptualise it, is going through a period of change, and also highlights a potential divide in the form that our explanations and descriptions of police culture take. To some, therefore, police culture is a phenomenon that, through targeted action, initiatives and policies, can be addressed and subsequently modified. These approaches are fundamentally reformist and provide a means of addressing the manifestations of police culture (for example, negative or discriminatory behaviours) without really engaging too explicitly with the subtleties of the culture itself. On the other hand, argues Loftus, explanations have been developed that present a much more diverse conception of the nature and properties of police culture and one that is predicated on differences in culture and behaviour rather than similarity. The idea of police culture, therefore, has been replaced by one of police cultures. These different sets of explanations have meant that more established thinking about police culture has generally fallen out of favour, leading to a variety of ways of thinking about what police culture is, how it works and how best to investigate it. In what some might consider a telling affirmation of the cyclical nature of intellectual ideas, Loftus, while acknowledging the contribution made by those authors who emphasise difference above continuity at a cultural level, makes a persuasive case to argue that there is sufficient universality between police cultures for us to continue to refer to them in the singular. One of the largest challenges that faces us, and one that is made explicit by Loftus's work, is that culture impacts broadly and at many levels within a police context. While management initiatives to modify or even replace culture may be deemed successful by virtue of them causing a change in expressed behaviour, it might be premature to hail these as successful instances of cultural change. Cultural artefacts or manifestations and underlying cultural beliefs are, as organisational theorists such as Schein make clear, essentially different. Evidence of cultural change being driven by new initiatives may therefore be misleading and may represent behavioural but not attitudinal change. Furthermore, such changes may be driven by external pressures such as the recognition of formerly marginalised groups, and when one focuses on less politicised dimensions, such as class, we may find that little effort has been made by police institutions to address these at the structural, let alone the behavioural or attitudinal, level.

Questions for further consideration

1. Consider the explanations of police behaviour put forward in the Scarman and Macpherson reports. Which of the two reports do you find to present the most effective explanation of police racism? Why?
2. How can we account for the apparent prevalence of masculine values in policing? How do these impact on (a) the public and (b) the police organisation?
3. Reflect on why the significance of social class to police culture receives relatively little attention.

Further reading

Brown, J. (2007) 'From cult of masculinity to smart macho: Gender perspectives on police occupational culture', in M. O'Neill, M. Marks and A. Singh (eds) *Police Occupational Culture: New Debates and Directions*, New York: Elsevier, pp 205–26.

Macpherson, W. (1999) *The Stephen Lawrence Inquiry*, Cm 4262, London: HMSO.

Scarman, G. (1982) *The Scarman Report: The Brixton Disorders 10–12 April 1981*, London: Pelican.

5

Police culture and leadership

This chapter will address the challenges of both applying the concept of culture to police leaders and the challenges faced by police leaders in terms of managing police culture. In particular, attention will be drawn to the existence of multiple cultures, of tensions between management and operational cultures and cultural resistance to leadership agendas. In doing so, this chapter will draw on my work (Cockcroft, 2019), which sets out these particular themes as a way of extending our knowledge of the relationship between police culture and police leadership. These topics will be contextualised in respect of the new public management (NPM) agenda and its impact on policing over recent years.

For many years, the relationship between police culture and police leadership failed to attract systematic attention from academics, with early work into police culture tending to focus on the interactions between lower-ranking police officers and civilians. In this regard, police culture essentially focused on the values, attitudes and behaviours of officers towards their external audience, the public, and the cultural dynamics as played out within the rank structure of the organisation were subjected to substantially less scrutiny. On those occasions where academics did explore the role that culture played in shaping internal relations between groups of officers this was likely to focus on either the divide between management and 'street'-level officers (see Reuss-Ianni and Ianni, 1983) or between different roles (see Manning, 1993). Over time, however, the link between police culture and leadership has received more attention, and this has facilitated a greater understanding of the challenges for police organisations of implementing strategic decisions at the operational level. It is probably helpful here to clarify the distinction between police management and police leadership. Police management tends to relate to the direct relationship between street police officers and their line management. Police leadership, on the other hand, refers to the more strategic direction given to policing by those in senior positions, and this has become more central to debates in policing over recent years.

Increasingly, the interest in police culture as a determinant of the police–public relationship has been balanced by a growing focus on how the lower police ranks respond to police leadership and the strategic direction provided by it. This emphasis has gained momentum largely because leadership has become associated with cultural change (Cockcroft, 2014). One example that will help to illustrate this idea is from William Bratton, the US police chief who undertook senior police leadership roles in a range of US cities and was tipped by some as a viable choice for Commissioner of the London Metropolitan Police in the wake of the London riots of 2011. In an interview with *The Guardian* newspaper at the time, Bratton proclaimed that 'I think of myself as a transformational leader who changes cultures' (quoted in Dodd and Stratton, 2011). Such sentiments help to reinforce the essentially negative view with which police culture is regarded and, furthermore, show that this view is shared by the police at the strategic level.

This is also particularly illuminating in what it tells us about the role of leadership in modern police organisations. The emergence of NPM has aided in embedding this notion that police leadership has become synonymous with the management and change of unprofessional and ineffective working cultures, especially for those aspiring officers wishing to progress their career (FitzGerald et al, 2002). The College of Policing's *Leadership Review* (2015) appeared to reinforce this idea that police culture had a fundamentally negative effect when it identified police occupational culture as one of the six key areas of policing that needed to undergo change, as a means of responding to the contemporary challenges of financial austerity and perceived reductions in police legitimacy.

To fully engage with this issue, it is important to understand the ways in which policing has been structured in respect of its managerial ethos. Prior to the early 1980s, policing attracted little attention or commentary in respect of which management model could be most appropriately applied to it. However, by the 1980s, we were witnessing a quiet revolution in the underlying ethos of public sector institutions, particularly in respect of the value they provide to the taxpayer. In 1983, Home Office Circular 114/83 'Manpower, Effectiveness and Efficiency in the Police Service' was circulated, and this set the tone for future developments in this area and, in particular, laid the foundations for the Sheehy report of 1993, which re-focused the policing sector in the UK onto the three 'E's' of economy, effectiveness and efficiency. From this point on, police forces were increasingly held to account to prove that they were delivering value, and this was underpinned by a regime of performance indicators, audits and inspections. This impetus revitalised the way in which leadership was framed within the policing context, and attempted to supersede traditional models of public sector management with ideas derived from the private sector (and more directly focused on tangible 'costs' rather than more abstract 'value'). This model prospered despite changes in government (with power shifting from Conservative to Labour in 1997), with the Local Government Act of 1999 (Golding and Savage, 2008) continuing this approach to police management. Jacques de Maillard and Stephen Savage (2018) note that, despite the many challenges associated with these measures and the cynicism with which they continue to be viewed, these managerial ideals continue to be popular among policy makers.

Chief constables

Looking at the role of the chief constable, it is possible to chart evidence that supports the idea that this period of NPM, which emerged in the early 1990s, has fundamentally altered the ways in which they lead. In particular, Robert Reiner's (1992b) work into understanding how chief constables operate identified a number of different forms of 'ideal type' of leadership style. These he categorised as the 'Baron', 'Bobby', 'Boss' and 'Bureaucrat'. It is interesting that, if one compares Reiner's work to the next major work assessing the ways in which senior leaders within the police operate (Bryn Caless's 2011 *Policing at the Top*), the style of 'Bureaucratic' leadership has become the most widespread type of management within the police, and this has paralleled the rise of private sector management models within the police. However, we should be cautious before concluding that the paradigm shift in public organisations has led to a wholesale bureaucratic revolution in policing. After all, Caless's work also appeared to identify 'considerable pessimism among chief officers about the nature of leadership in the police and about what its constituents should be ... there is little unity on what constitutes a successful police leader and even less on whether such attributes can be taught' (2011: 117). Obviously, therefore, police leadership is a far from straightforward concept in respect of how it works in practice.

Above, we looked very briefly at Reiner's (1992b) work and identified the cultural types that he saw chief constables as adhering to. It is worth exploring these cultural styles (what Reiner called 'ideal-typical patterns', 1992b: 303) in greater depth. To Reiner, the similarity in the challenges faced by senior officers and the commonality of their career experiences led to generalised responses, and it is these that Reiner views as creating the 'dominant culture' (1992b: 303) of chief constables. His use of different types of category is interesting in that it allows for variations around these embedded cultural themes and, while these are unlikely to fully reflect the reality of those officers' experience, they allow us to understand those core factors that influence responses at the individual level. Underpinning the four categories of working style proposed by Reiner are four key factors: 'period', 'problems', 'place' and 'pedigree' (Cockcroft, 2019). The first, 'period', refers to the fact that cultural typologies of senior officers are in part determined by the external influences that impact on that level of leadership at that particular time. In Reiner's work, for example, which, of course, very much echoed the period in which he wrote, reference is made to the concept of post-Scarmanism (1992b: 304), which drew on the recommendations of Lord Scarman's report into the inner-city disturbances of the early 1980s and the impact of diversity considerations on the work of the police (Cockcroft, 2019). Likewise, a more contemporary example of such a period-specific pressure might be that of EBP, which is increasingly exerting influence over the strategic direction taken by senior officers. The second factor identified by Reiner is 'problems'. The specific difficulties faced by chief constables, according to Reiner, will influence the way they respond to a range of issues. These can be national or local in character and will impact on and influence, to a greater or lesser extent, the style which that chief constable adopts. To Reiner's sample, key challenges included quite specific forms of unrest such as the miners' strike but also some more generalised apprehension around legislative developments (such as the introduction of the Police and Criminal Evidence Act in 1984). Of note here is that some issues might transcend specific historic periods. For example, the disquiet presented by Reiner's sample in respect of the Financial Management Initiative (FMI), which introduced greater financial controls across the public sector, are echoed in today's concerns regarding ongoing funding reductions. For example, in September 2018 the BBC reported Bill Skelly, Chief Constable of Lincolnshire Police, voicing concerns regarding budget reductions in the force. In the article, Skelly reported that the need to find savings of £16.8 million over three years was likely to lead to staff reductions of 60 police officers, 30 civilian staff and 53 police community support officers (BBC News, 2018). Such challenges are likely to become more longstanding causes of concern to police forces over future years, and will tend to have similar impacts on a number of forces. The third factor highlighted by Reiner is that of 'place', and he refers to the 'social and physical ecology, the political structure and culture, the ethnic mix, the economic condition' (1992b: 305) of the particular external environment within which the chief constable operates. One of the key determinants impacting such issues is whether or not the organisation is a large urban police force or a smaller, more rural, constabulary. As the work of Jan Terpstra (2017) shows, such geographic distinctions between city and country police forces impact culturally on the outlook of rank and file officers and can promote very different conceptions of the police role and the skills required by police officers to be considered competent in their role. To Reiner, such cultural distinctions also impact those officers in senior positions. Finally, Reiner draws attention to the importance of 'pedigree' in helping to determine the cultural disposition of senior police officers. The background and experience of senior officers will shape their basic personal disposition towards police work, and this will be mediated through pressures linked to period, problems and place to create a particular occupational outlook.

As mentioned previously, the above factors interact and combine to produce four separate types of senior police officer, which, while not intended to fully mirror real-life examples, nevertheless provide a yardstick through which to understand similarities and differences in the outlook of senior officers. The 'Baron' category refers to a senior officer of middle-class origins leading a county force. 'Barons' were typified as having military experience and a predominantly operational rather than administrative focus. Such leaders saw a primary role of the police as to facilitate informal control within relatively low-crime communities. This category of leader tended to voice concern at both the increased politicisation of the policing arena and the tendency towards centralised intervention into local police matters. The 'Bobby' category invokes the spirit of the Golden Age of British policing by depicting a police leader who is working class and leads a force with both urban and rural areas centred on a principal city. This category of leader is very much a proponent of traditional policing methods and was drawn to the job by its variety and the opportunity to work with a broad range of people. The 'Bobby' is very much steeped in operational, rather than administrative, police work, and resents external influences (emanating from either politicians or civil servants) impacting on their ability to respond to the wishes of the local population. Reiner's third typology, the 'Boss', is very much similar to the 'Bobby' in overall outlook. However, his or her disposition is much shaped by their geographical location, typically an urban area with substantial crime issues. Again with a traditional working-class background, the 'Boss' sees the police as the thin blue line separating society from a rising tide of crime and disorder. The local challenges they face tend to make them, perhaps a little reluctantly, proponents of reactive police work. The final typology proposed by Reiner, the 'Bureaucrat', represents a hybrid form bridging the tradition associated with the 'Bobby' tempered with both an affinity for, and a mastery of, contemporary management styles. This balance allows the 'Bureaucrat' to display a sympathetic and diplomatic front to officers on the front line while building legitimacy among local communities. Simultaneously, this style of leader proves highly adept at internalising, disseminating and implementing whatever contemporary messages are emanating from police central leadership.

Police leadership

One of the challenges of understanding police leadership in a contemporary sense is that recent years have witnessed a substantial growth in the academic study of leadership. This somewhat broad concept has been central to many of our debates about organisations, how people work within organisational contexts and how we can modify behaviour to ensure that organisations are more effective (whatever the measure of that effectiveness might be). While this expansion of the knowledge base is to be welcomed, as it signals the fact that we are learning more about how leadership works and of how to apply it to different contexts, it does create challenges, especially when one tries to apply it to the area of policing.

Discussions of leadership tend to begin with an assumption that staff behaviour among the lower ranks is in need of modification, and that the cause of poor or unprofessional police work is essentially a problem of police culture. To be specific, the notion rests on the idea that not only is the culture of the police responsible for promoting negative attitudes but also, and importantly, that there is an unproblematic relationship between culture and behaviour. That is to say, there exists an assumption that police officers unfailingly act in accordance with their occupational culture, therefore signalling that we can draw a causal link from culture to behaviour. This rather simplistic view of the relationship between culture and police behaviour has become increasingly embedded in the discourse of police leadership (Cockcroft, 2019).

When we turn our attention towards the idea of how the higher ranks lead, there is substantial evidence to suggest that they have traditionally adopted styles of leadership that fail to engage positively with their officers (Cockcroft, 2019). In 1998, Michel Girodo carried out survey research with police leaders from police organisations throughout the world to ascertain the forms of leadership they utilised. What Girodo found was that, while a range of different leadership styles existed (characterised as 'Machiavellian', 'transformational', 'bureaucratic' and 'social contract'), police leaders tended to adopt the Machiavellian approach. This leadership style, according to John Krimmel and Paul Lindenmuth (2001), is one that is founded on a somewhat ruthless and manipulative approach to leadership which creates a negative relationship between leaders and their staff. Furthermore, John Keane and Peter Bell (2014) highlight the ways in which Machiavellian forms of leadership are, in some cases, associated with police corruption at leadership levels. An interesting finding which emerges from research into this subject is that, despite the apparent prevalence of Machiavellian leadership styles in policing, police leaders are often favourable to more positive ways of leading but feel that their organisations are unsupportive of such management styles. This itself points to potential structural issues inhibiting management and leadership reform.

Leadership is also intricately related to the concept of culture in that, apart from 'good' leadership being seen as an antidote or panacea to the 'problem' of police culture, particular leadership styles are also seen as causing some of the challenges faced by police organisations. The more negative forms of police leadership, such as Machiavellian or bureaucratic types, lead to a range of adverse impacts that can severely disadvantage police organisations. Such features include low staff morale, high turnover of staff, poor quality relations between management and lower-ranking officers and a largely self-interested workforce.

Recent years have seen a significant increase in the amount of interest accorded to participatory or transformational leadership styles in policing (Cockcroft, 2014). Transformational leadership was popularised by writers like Bernard Bass and Bruce Avolio (1993) and refers to styles of leadership that reject the bureaucratic and Machiavellian forms. The latter they refer to as transactional (rather than transformational), where the relationships between leader and worker are reduced to transactional arrangements whereby one gets rewarded for displaying certain forms of behaviour and punished for acting in ways that go against the expectations of the management. Such leadership styles are criticised for advocating reductive relationships between managers and staff that are predicated on simple reward and punishment formulas. The issue here, according to Bass and Avolio (1993: 116), is that 'contractual relationships' are central to the relationship between leaders and workers. As a result, the relationship between the organisation and the worker is simplistic, and the latter invests little if any emotional energy in the organisation.

Transformational leadership, however, adopts a markedly different approach. Rather than merely stipulating the conditions under which a worker's actions will be met with reward or, alternatively, punishment, transformational approaches reject the transactional element of the relationship and seek to make it transformative by basing it on principles, according to Marisa Silvestri (2007: 39), of 'participation, consultation and inclusion'. Under this model, police officers carry out the will of their leader not because they wish to maximise reward or to avoid punishment but because they fully subscribe to the organisation's strategy and see the proposed action as the best possible option.

While it might appear that transformational approaches to leadership present a natural and somewhat obvious fit for the organisational solutions required by the police, I draw attention to problems with such assumptions on the grounds of cultural plurality (Cockcroft, 2014). I suggest that one of the key challenges of transformational leadership as a means of managing the culture of the police is that, increasingly, academics are very much accepting of the idea of cultural plurality – that police culture is fluid and ever-changing and, importantly, that this leads to numerous police cultures. While a particular leadership style might be an effective means of mitigating against the impact or effects of a set of behaviours or values linked to a specific or discernible set of cultural influences, it is difficult to assess how we can direct police leadership to effectively engage with numerous, and, perhaps, contradictory, cultural forces. Furthermore, organisations are environments in which different cultural forces get played out at both the organisational and occupational levels. While these terms are sometimes used interchangeably, they do refer to different cultural forces that operate in essentially different ways. Again, this does draw us to the idea that the notion of a single discernible police culture is problematic.

It might be helpful here to expand on the previous point regarding organisational and occupational culture. When exploring the cultural world of police officers, although there are occasions when we might look at organisational culture (for example, when exploring some areas pertaining to senior leadership), we naturally tend to cast our focus towards the occupational culture. The reason for this will be identified shortly, after the distinction between occupational and organisational culture has been made. If we use the concept of organisational culture to explore the behaviour of employees within a particular organisation, we are making an assumption about the foundation of the cultural identity that has been adopted, specifically in that their cultural identity is tied to the organisation or body that employs them. Such an approach is liable to over-predict the extent to which workers identify with their employing organisation. Instead, a strong case can be made to suggest that workers culturally align themselves more strongly with the values of their occupation than their organisation. A good example of this is a piece of research undertaken by Kathleen Gregory (1983). Gregory's focus was the application of ideas about organisational and occupational culture and how it related to those people employed as technical specialists within the Californian computing industry. The research found that the primary driver of the working values and culture adopted by these workers was not so much the culture of the organisation for which they worked but rather the cultural identity that surrounded the specific role they undertook. In Gregory's study, engineers and scientists within particular organisations had very different approaches to their work, the implication being therefore that engineers and scientists culturally identified with their role rather than the organisation they worked for. When we transpose this to the police, we find that police officers tend to identify with values that are compatible with the role they hold within the occupation rather than those of the organisation. This distinction is helpful in that it allows us to understand those research findings which suggest that a multiplicity of cultures exist (for example, Chan, 1997), that different values exist between management and non-management officers (for example, Reuss-Ianni and Ianni, 1983), and that different roles within the police adopt different sets of values (for example, Manning, 1993). Indeed, Gregory's work, placed in the context of the sheer breadth of roles that exist in modern policing, provides strong evidence to support the idea that a plurality of cultures exists within organisations. A further distinction is made by Eugene Paoline (2003), who suggests that organisational culture is top-down (that is, is forced on workers from the leadership level of the organisation), whereas occupational culture works in the opposite direction and is sustained from the lower ranks. This idea works well in the context of what knowledge we have about police culture and its relationship to leadership. Research into police culture is usually conducted among the lower ranks and is often viewed as related to the challenges associated with delivering professional operational policing in public-facing roles. Organisational culture, however, essentially provides a more corporate and formally aligned set of values. Furthermore, we can use research conducted into police unionism (see Cockcroft, 2019) as a means of exploring the views of those officers at the 'grass-roots' level and their antagonism with the leadership styles at the top of the organisation. Monique Marks's (2007) work in this area is particularly helpful. She found that police unions have mobilised the support of officers in the lower ranks to oppose elements of the new forms of management that have emerged in recent decades. She notes that 'Police unions will always present a challenge from below, but since union members identify themselves primarily as police officers so too their union culture will always have a strong affinity with the umbrella culture of the police organisation' (Marks, 2007: 247).

At the same time, the unions have promoted a discourse of policing that is very much based on traditional ideas of policing which draw on the symbolism of the Golden Age of policing. Evidence for this comes from the Police Federation's #CutsHaveConsequences campaign (see, for example, Metropolitan Police Federation, 2015), which highlights the impact of austerity on police budgets. The general focus of this campaign was used to highlight the impact of cuts not to leadership roles or civilian staff but on operational policing, especially those roles that interact directly with communities. In doing so, the campaign reinforced the idea that it is these roles, those at the lower end of the rank structure, which constitute 'proper' police work and which provide security to the public. In turn, these very traditionally themed campaigns reinforce concerns, as highlighted by Michael Rowe (2006), that substantial anxieties exist surrounding the gradual erosion of the cornerstone of police work, that of the traditional street-level police officer role.

At this point, it might be helpful to pause and reflect on the extent to which this set of cultural tensions between police leaders and the rank and file is embedded or intractable. Despite this apparent conflict at a cultural level, there does appear to be a certain degree of scope for change (Cockcroft, 2019). First, I argue, it is increasingly the case that leadership is not viewed as being solely a characteristic of the senior roles within the police, and there is an emerging expectation that leadership qualities should be an integral element of all police roles (see, for example, Grint and Thornton, 2015). Second, these changes are making it easier for the traditional cultural values of the police to be challenged, thus increasing the scope for cultural fluidity. Third, policing at all ranks is being influenced by external pressures that have drawn the police away from the crime fighting stereotypes of earlier generations, with the result that the service elements of policing are increasingly being viewed as legitimate by both male and female police officers. Finally, the growing diversity of police recruits (along lines of gender, ethnic background, class and educational level) have tended to dilute the traditional rigidity of the mindset of the average officer. It might indeed be the case that the changes, charted above, are increasingly facilitated, quite simply, by the fact that the managerial context that emerged in the late 20th century has ceased to be a 'new' element of the police world. As its novelty wears thin, it will cease to provoke the levels of cultural resistance that we have seen. As Pat O'Malley and Steven Hutchinson (2007: 170, cited in Cockcroft, 2019) note,

> New generations entering the police "service" may no longer regard the managerial principles, and the competitive market structures associated with it, as alien or out of place. For better or worse, this environment has been becoming part of everyday life for two decades, reaching into many institutions – long enough for it to become fairly "normal" rather than "new".

Managing performance

While it might be the case that, in years to come, the use of managerialist mechanisms, as suggested by O'Malley and Hutchinson (2007), will become part of the accepted policing landscape, at present there does appear to be a degree of resistance directed towards the imposition of management styles that are not seen as reflecting traditional police culture values. For example, a paper by myself and Iain Beattie (2009) explored the experiences, in a British police organisation, of implementing a new management performance regime that allocated points to officers for engaging in particular behaviours, an approach essentially founded on transactional leadership styles. In our coverage of views of these changes, lower-ranking officers' responses provided some insight into how they perceived the police role, and facilitated some understanding of the ways in which police culture and leadership approaches conflict. The first theme to emerge was that of the challenge of police performance analysis or, in other words, the difficulties with developing leadership approaches and management tools that actually reflect the work that officers do. This research found that officers identified the challenges of reassurance and community policing, which, while valuable, prove difficult to quantify in respect of measures of police performance. One particular officer went further and suggested that, under the system being studied, reassurance work within the community would not only fail to accrue points but also indicate 'poor performance' (Cockcroft and Beattie, 2009: 532). Officers saw the mechanism as being weighted towards administrative skills and form-filling rather than providing discernible benefits to the community being policed. The officers who tended to engage with the system were either new officers or members of the management ranks. Lower-ranking officers with substantial length of service reported the mechanism as having no substantive impact on the style of policing they used, and also reported not even reviewing the points that they had accrued under the system. This signalled a lack of engagement with what was viewed as an arbitrary system for measuring and assessing effectiveness. The second key theme was that of data corruption, which suggested that some officers 'game played' the system to accrue points and others expressed concern at the ways in which the system introduced a level of competitiveness between officers and teams. One example of this is where a patrol shift failed to pass on intelligence to the incoming shift as they were concerned that the later shift would be allocated the points that would be distributed as a result of any actions based on that information. Another example saw a victim of an assault left unattended while officers concentrated their attentions on apprehending the assailant so as to secure the points that were available for the arrest. As one police officer told us, '... we'd do things we weren't meant to do, go to the crime car and say, "got any arrests, got any quick bodies?" and we'd end up arresting a fourteen year old for nicking a fiver's worth of sweets' (quoted in Cockcroft and Beattie, 2009: 533). Similarly, officers reported other techniques to maximise 'performance'. One stated that congregating youths who would previously have been dispersed using informal means would now be arrested for causing a disturbance. Likewise, those officers who understood the intricate mechanics of the performance mechanism knew that they could actually accrue more points by stopping seven people rather than arresting four (Cockcroft and Beattie, 2009).

A number of issues arise from this research that allow us to explore the relationship between leadership and culture. First, there is the negative impact of what Ronnie Flanagan (2008: 49) referred to as 'heavily bureaucratic processes' that have become common in police organisations. An example of this would be the rigidified performance measurement mechanism detailed in our research (Cockcroft and Beattie, 2009). Such processes are problematic to Flanagan as they are related to the fact that police professional discretion has been eroded over recent years. Professional discretion (the power to make decisions, within acceptable parameters, as a situation dictates), while central to the idea of police culture, has, over recent years, been targeted by police management initiatives as a problematic source of 'bad' decisions. Second, these processes tend to de-motivate some officers and reinforce the cynicism with which many officers view police management. One officer interviewed in our research stated, with regard to performance measurement, that 'it's bollocks ... when you're dealing with people who are stabbed, you don't need points' (Cockcroft and Beattie, 2009: 532). Interestingly, the HMIC (1999) paper on police integrity reinforced the implication of the above quotation when it noted that performance cultures had, in some cases, a considerable negative impact on police integrity. Third, there was a concern that performance cultures were apparently reshaping the police role in ways that failed to reflect the range of tasks undertaken by police officers, leading to the manufacture of, at best, inaccurate and, at worst, meaningless data that played down the importance of the service element of police work. In short, rather than measure police performance, there is an implicit, although rarely articulated, expectation that police performance mechanisms actually shape the behaviour of officers in ways that make them prioritise some tasks (those that are easy to measure) at the expense of others (those that are difficult to measure).

A substantial focus of recent work into police leadership has therefore been the performance culture. This is a result of police forces trying to ensure that police behaviour is directed towards engaging with those elements of their role that will have the most measurable or demonstrable impact. Where police leaders attempted to renegotiate the core tasks of police work, as we evidenced (Cockcroft and Beattie, 2009), a substantial amount of cultural resistance was generated. Fundamentally, the conflict appeared to be centred on the apparent attempt to reduce the amount of discretion available to police officers. From the officers' perspective, such moves were cynical attempts to reduce the range of police work that they considered important to those that could easily translate into quantifiable data. The message is clear, that some front-line officers feel that they should be able to determine the form that policing takes, rather than managers whom they perceive as removed from day-to-day knowledge and experience of police work.

The distinction between organisational and occupational culture and the existence of a plurality of role-defined cultures yet again lead us towards the inescapable complexity of police culture. Although police leadership is often presented as a somewhat straightforward solution to the issue of police culture, we are posed with some quite critical challenges. For example, how does leadership effectively engage with culture where there is not one discernible culture but numerous cultures within an organisation derived from different roles, ranks and personal characteristics?

Some of these issues, it should be noted, were identified by research undertaken as far back as the 1960s, sharing some parallels, for example, with the ideas of James Q. Wilson (1968) in his book *Varieties of Police Behavior: The Management of Law and Order in Eight Communities*. In this work, the author differentiated between three different styles of policing that he had identified in his research conducted in the US. The first type he identified, the 'Watchman' style, focused on order maintenance as the core role of the police, meaning that some disorder (such as that associated with 'victimless' crimes) was tolerated. The second identified approach to policing, the 'Legalistic' style, represented a form of policing centred around the universal application of the law and where discretion in such processes was not tolerated. The third and final approach was the 'Service' style, which saw the law enforcement element of police work taking a lower priority to the service role. This style was adopted in middle-class communities where the threat of crime and disorder was generally associated with 'outsiders' and juveniles. Central to Wilson's work was that these styles of policing emerged as a result of management instruction. What we find, as a result, is that, historically at least, variations in leadership style could contribute to the development of quite different approaches to policing which, one might assume, promote different cultural values and ways of thinking about policing.

In conclusion, and as Caless's (2011) work suggests, we may be witnessing a narrowing of the styles of leadership available to senior officers and this may, as a result, limit the opportunities to implement different styles of police work. At the same time, the positioning by the College of Policing, in its 2015 *Leadership Review*, of police culture as an essentially negative concept does suggest that a particularly singular view of culture is being promoted at present at the strategic level. While this no doubt allows police leadership to articulate the scope of the problems facing policing in a direct and unambiguous way, it does little to suggest that culture is being addressed in a meaningful manner or one that fully displays an understanding of its scope and characteristics. Part of the explanation behind this may be the essentially politicised divide between leadership and grass-roots conceptions of policing that we can see through the work of academics such as Marks (2007) and through initiatives such as the #CutsHaveConsequences campaign promoted by professional associations. While the relationship between police leadership and police culture continues to be interwoven within wider contexts of politics, professionalisation agendas and resourcing restrictions, straightforward explanations are unlikely to be immediately forthcoming.

Questions for further consideration

1. Discuss the implication of the following statement made by Bill Bratton, US police chief: 'I think of myself as a transformational leader who changes cultures' (quoted in Dodd and Stratton, 2011).
2. Consider the different priorities that lower-ranking police officers and their leaders will have. How do you think these will impact, if at all, on their cultural values?

Further reading

Cockcroft, T. (2019) 'Police culture and police leadership', in P. Ramshaw, M. Silvestri and M. Simpson (eds) *Police Leadership: Changing Landscapes*, London: Palgrave.

College of Policing (2015) *Leadership Review: Recommendations for Delivering Leadership at All Levels*, London: College of Policing, Available from: www.college.police.uk/What-we-do/Development/ Promotion/the-leadership-review/Pages/The-Leadership-Review. aspx

6

Police culture and
the police role

This chapter will address the fundamental relationship between the work roles of the police and the cultural dynamics associated with police organisations. This principle will be used to explore work that sees the cultural world of police officers as intrinsically determined by the roles that they engage in. In this way, the book will explore cultural similarity and difference between police officers working in different roles and contexts to explore the tension between ideas of singular and plural cultures.

To understand the idea of police culture we need to be aware of the ways in which culturally determined police values, attitudes and behaviours are shaped by the specific roles that police officers undertake, and the way that these sit against the wider external context of a particular society. At times, it can appear that a somewhat simplistic juxtaposition exists in respect of our understanding of police culture whereby the mere act of joining a police organisation as an officer denotes exposure to, and internalisation of, a specific set of assumptions that will dictate not only the ways in which that officer sees the world but also how they interact with it. This apparent convention was the orthodox way of understanding police culture for many years and can be attributed to a number of factors, all related to the idea that there is one, relatively distinct, police culture.

Traditional focus on lower-rank policing

The sociological study of police work was, for many years, research into lower-ranking police officers undertaking patrol work in problematic metropolitan areas. In this way, police culture became synonymous with the challenges posed for the police by routine activities undertaken by patrol officers. Similarly, much of the early research was driven by the specific concerns of that era, for example the policing of minority ethnic populations, and the findings of the research did little to dispel such perceptions. Accordingly, we can identify the relevance of David Sklansky's idea of 'cognitive burn-in' (2007: 20), where he suggests that we should concern ourselves not only with the resistance of police culture to change but also with the reluctance of academics to rethink the assumptions that they hold. In particular, he suggests that these academic assumptions can be compared to the psychological concept of schema. It is probably worthwhile, at this point, to briefly address this concept. According to Hiroko Nishida (1999), individuals, when faced with a familiar situation, will draw on knowledge that they have used previously. These 'generalized collections of knowledge' (1999: 402) are not homogenous in nature and can work at the individual level, in a very personal and individualised way, or at a cultural level, where every member of a particular culture will utilise that schema, or even at a universal level, where all members of a society share such knowledge. Some academics have therefore found it helpful to use the concept to explain the cultural knowledge that police officers draw on. Rachel Venema (2014) draws on the concept of schema to explain how police officers use existing knowledge to make decisions regarding the categorisation of sexual assault reports when deciding whether, for example, to classify them as either false or, alternatively, as legitimate. Here, however, Sklansky uses the term to explain how academics conceptualise police culture through recycling and reusing ideas that were originally used decades earlier by academics researching this area. As Sklansky is quick to point out, however, both society and police work have undergone extensive change in the intervening years, and the application of established schema to substantially different contexts of society and police work might be problematic. Furthermore, he articulates concern that these substantially embedded ideas about police culture are not only inaccurate but also tend to obscure our ability to engage with other, more appropriate, ways of thinking about police work. In particular, the work of Peter Manning (2007) supports Sklansky's ideas about the use of established knowledge when studying police culture by drawing our attention to the largely simplistic ways in which both police work and its culture are portrayed. Two key assumptions are questioned by Manning. First, that the key focus of police work is crime and, second, that the occupational culture of the police is essentially drawn from working-class conceptions of masculinity. The criticisms put forward by Sklansky and Manning remain a helpful starting point towards developing a critical understanding of police culture and the limitations that have emerged in relation to some of the earlier work in this area.

At the same time, it is not difficult to understand why these schemata exist. In terms of the predominant focus on street-level police work, in the years pre-dating the current widespread collaboration between police organisations and universities (see Goode and Lumsden, 2018), gaining access to police forces for the purpose of research was a challenging undertaking (see, for example, Fox and Lundman, 1974). Furthermore, it was unlikely that requests to observe the less visible and less public-facing areas of police work would be granted by police organisations. Likewise, much of the early work into police culture was being conducted at a time when, according to Robert Reiner and Tim Newburn (2007), police research was operating under ideologically driven agendas (the 'controversy' agenda, followed by the 'conflict' agenda), which tended to focus on negative experiences of police work reported by members of the public. Inevitably, this drew attention to the elements of policing based on interaction with the public and, therefore, to concerns over the publicly visible policing carried out by lower-ranking officers. Even if one starts looking at the somewhat niche area of police narratives and storytelling (see, for example, Shearing and Ericson, 1991; van Hulst, 2014), one can discern very little sense of the language and discourses of police jargon extending beyond that of street-level officers. Likewise, in one of the early classics in this field, Jerome Skolnick's *Justice Without Trial* (1994), there is an explanatory framework that reduces the reasons for the existence of a police working personality down to the three elements of danger, authority and effectiveness. It can be argued that this helpful, if quite broad, conceptualisation of the drivers of police culture implicitly suggests a singular culture, failing as it does to differentiate between the impact of different levels of these three factors or, in fact, the existence of other variables. It is reasonably safe to argue, therefore, that the predominant position in police studies has been to conceive of police culture as a generic and universal concept that applies to all elements of all police organisations, despite being founded on research undertaken mainly with lower-ranking officers.

It is important to address this point as it allows us, first, to explain and understand the reason why much of the early work in this area might appear somewhat narrow in focus, deterministic and restricted in explaining a broad array of behaviour and attitudes. Similarly, the adoption of a generic schema surrounding police culture has allowed it to become a rather blunt tool when it comes to explaining what the police do. Traditional visions of police culture that view it as an over-powering force that impacts negatively on the world view of police officers, regardless of their individual characteristics, their background, their prior experience or their rank, are liable to experience difficulty in providing a meaningful description or explanation of the contemporary cultural world of the police.

The changing context of policing

Before addressing the specific impact of role differentiation on the cultural determinants of policing, it is probably necessary to remind ourselves of the substantial amount of change that has beset the police over recent years. Trevor Jones and Tim Newburn (2002) identify some of the areas that might signal that policing has been transformed over recent decades. The first of these is the growth of policing services outside the public sector, which effectively suggests an end to the state's monopoly over security. The second is the increasingly globalised character of policing as our security needs expand to cover threats that are transnational in nature. The third refers to new ways of managing police organisations as the public sector has increasingly adopted business models based on private sector practice. The fourth refers to the increasing use by police organisations of technological solutions to crime and order control. Finally, Jones and Newburn (2002) refer to the growing use of 'risk' as a central theme in how the police organise their security delivery. And while they underplay the degree to which these changes represent a wholesale change to policing (and the extent to which they can be considered change in global terms), they acknowledge that, to many observers, these transformations represent a new form of public policing. Since Jones and Newburn's work was published it may also be possible to identify other emerging issues that have impacted on the breadth and nature of police work. Recent years have seen the growth of cybercrime as a major challenge for the police (see HMIC, 2015), growing debates about what constitutes knowledge within policing (see Wood et al, 2017), dialogue surrounding policing and higher education (see Hallenberg and Cockcroft, 2017), and evidence for the emergence of new and different forms of police culture (see Charman, 2017). These areas represent just a small sample of the changes that have been identified in policing, its culture and the way in which academics understand the relationship between the two.

Role differentiation and police culture

Furthermore, prior to the changes we have witnessed over recent decades and that are identified above, there was scope to explore the way in which culture was related to the specific roles within the police. As far back as the late 1960s, Arthur Niederhoffer (1969) identified tensions between the professionalised cultures of middle-class police managers and the more unionised cultures of working-class patrol officers. For Elizabeth Reuss-Ianni and Francis Ianni (1983), lower-ranking police officers' working personalities were determined by the values of their police precinct or police station, which amounted to '... a distinctive and distinct social system' (1983: 252, cited in Cockcroft, 2019), whereas the culture of the management and leadership ranks tended to be strongly influenced by external social dynamics and political forces. Similarly, Reiner (1992b), in his research into chief constables, identified very different drivers of working personality to those identified by Skolnick (1994) in his investigation based on patrol officers (Cockcroft, 2019). Furthermore, the work of Janet Chan (1997) also allowed for different cultural attributes in officers whose roles had different functions, a finding supported by Manning (1993), who identified three different cultures within the police: 'command', 'middle management' and 'lower participants'. From the above, it appears relatively straightforward to surmise that the particular police role that one undertakes will impact on one's values and assumptions, and that this strongly suggests that cultural differentiation does occur.

We must, however, remain cautious about assuming that the characteristics of lower-ranking police roles have a degree of universality. In a fascinating piece of research, Velmer Burton et al (1993) examined the legal codes of every US state to ascertain the extent to which we could discern consistency between them in terms of states' expectations of police officers. They begin by drawing on the work of Manning (1977), who identified that a major challenge 'was the inability of the police to define a mandate that will minimize the inconsistent nature of their self expectations and the expectations of those they serve' (1977: 28, cited in Burton et al, 1993). As Burton et al (1993) show, police scholars have also drawn attention to several other factors that influence the orientation of the police role, in particular, 'type of community', 'local politics' and 'society'. While Burton et al note a disparity between what the police and the public view as the police role, their work is of interest as it shows very differing articulations, at the level of state legal code, as to the formal nature of that role. There is, of course, much chance for variation between a legally articulated role for the police and its reality in practice; however, it is interesting to see how the general expectation, at state level, of the police role is not consistent. In this piece of research, the authors identified a total of 16 broad tasks that constitute the police role, and that can be classed under three main categories: peacekeeping ('preserve peace', 'suppress riots', 'protect life', 'uphold law and order' and 'protect morals'), law enforcement ('enforce criminal laws', 'arrest', 'detect/prevent crime', 'enforce traffic laws', 'search and seize', 'execute warrants', 'issue citations' and 'prosecute offenders') and service ('assist citizens'). Out of 50 states, a considerable degree of variation emerged in respect of these prescribed police roles. For example, 44% of states mandated no other role for the police than those associated with law enforcement. Furthermore, only 6% of states prescribed that police officers should only undertake peacekeeping roles, although 48% combined this role with law enforcement roles. Finally, no state legislature required its officers to solely undertake a service role, although one state did mandate service roles in conjunction with law enforcement. These research findings prompt further questions, not least about how US states articulate the service element of the police role. Given that tasks which could broadly be defined as service in nature constitute such a large proportion of the police officer role, it is surprising that they are not formally articulated through state legal codes, which appear, in comparison, to strictly define the law enforcement elements of police work. As a result, Burton et al (1993) forward two questions. First, why, given the prevalence of service functions in operational policing, are they not mandated by law in all but one state? Second, why are service-related roles generally ignored by state legislatures? A number of potential answers, note Burton et al, can be identified. It has been argued, for example, that local police operations are rarely directly influenced by state-level legislation and therefore role definition at that level is of little consequence for policing on the ground. Similarly, it has been argued that emphasising the service element of policing might give the impression that a particular state jurisdiction is not sufficiently focused on law enforcement issues, and that might explain the wilful omission of the service role for state descriptions. While it has been noted above that state legislation is unlikely to have a direct impact on the form that operational policing takes, such formal articulations of the police role are obviously a reflection of localised political considerations. For example, as in the case of states underplaying the service element of the patrol officer role for fear of being perceived as soft on crime, such considerations will surely direct the style of operational policing if such issues remain of sufficient concern to influence the wording of the legal mandate. In particular, one can detect elements of this in James Q. Wilson's (1968) work, where he describes how legalistic styles of police work emerge in jurisdictions where law enforcement is prioritised. Where law enforcement is the operational police focus, Wilson shows how the scope for police officers to use discretion becomes diminished. This can be a particularly attractive proposition at the local political level as the adoption of such a model is seen as protecting the local police from the possibility of scandal. In areas that adopt such models, this style of policing will, in turn, shape the values of officers who work under it (Cockcroft, 2013).

Similarly, William Pelfrey (2004) noted the differences that existed between community police officers and traditional police officers. While community policing is often presented as a specific policing philosophy, its implementation can largely be seen to be fragmented. In part, this might be caused by the fact that, in an increasingly complex field that demands specialisation, the community police officer is a generalist role characterised by a broad array of skills. Pelfrey's work focused on a comparison of community police officers and motorised patrol officers, and found that there were strong similarities between the two groups in respect of their beliefs in traditional values of law enforcement. However, he also found that community police officers were significantly more likely to experience higher job satisfaction, to endorse different ways of undertaking police work and to perceive the impact of their work to be higher. While not pointing to a wholesale divide in cultural outlook between these two groups of officers, there does appear to be a significant divergence in respect of traditional cultural manifestations such as cynicism and pessimism (see Reiner, 2010). Likewise, the work of John Balenovich et al (2008) is similarly of interest in that it identifies the sometimes apparently contradictory nature of police work in respect of the balancing of two distinct roles, crime control and social welfare, and shows how this creates 'role conflict' (2008: 21). The focus of their research was those police officers who undertake roles which involve responding to domestic violence incidents and the influence of both 'job specific socialisation factors' (2008: 22) and external influences from the wider community on their outlook. The authors used focus group interviews with officers to identify three different orientations to work – the 'strict enforcer', 'service officer' and 'integrated investigator'. The first of these, the 'strict enforcer', was characterised by the adoption of a very legalistic approach to dealing with domestic violence incidents. This position is succinctly described by one of the police officers in the research, who stated, 'A detective is a detective. A social worker is a social worker' (quoted in Balenovich et al, 2008: 26). This can be contrasted with the 'service officer' role, which was very much driven by a social welfare agenda where the investigative elements were largely underplayed in contrast to a prioritisation of the victim's needs. Finally, the 'integrated investigator' represented a hybrid approach that recognised that responses to domestic violence incidents draw on both law enforcement and social welfare approaches. This differentiation of orientation to role does raise some interesting issues as it points towards different cultural orientations among officers. In doing so, it reminds us that, while we might expect officers in particular roles to adopt similar world views as a result of that work, there is also the possibility that cultural variations may occur among officers undertaking the same tasks. In Balenovich et al's (2008) work, several possible reasons for these substantial differences are identified. For example, for officers whose outlook was consistent with the 'strict enforcer' category, the authors suggest that training is probably the cause of this legalistic focus. Those whose approach reflected the 'service officer' category appeared to be motivated by a mixture of previous work experience and personal biography. One such officer, cited in their research, referred to the ways in which their background in social work gave them the necessary skills to provide the necessary support and assistance to those affected by domestic violence. Likewise, two officers who worked in ways consistent with the service role were motivated to do so as a result of personal experience of being a victim of domestic violence or of witnessing it within their own family background. To Balenovich et al (2008), the orientation to domestic violence that was most likely to lead to an effective resolution of a domestic violence situation was that of the 'integrated investigator'. These findings, when placed in the context of other police culture research, are interesting in that they make clear, that, although variation does occur, specific police roles, which might demand particular skills, can also lead to coherent and consistent cultural reference points that align with that position. Further evidence of this comes from Malcolm Young's (1991) account of the distinct cultural world occupied by those police officers who undertook, as Young himself did, detective work with a drug squad. Here, the 'marginal universe' (1991: 89) which he inhabited meant that he shed many of the cultural assumptions that he had previously been socialised with as they offered little relevance to the requirements of his present role. Likewise, Dick Hobbs's (1988) account of detective work in the East End of London shows how those officers cultivated an altogether more 'entrepreneurial' working culture than their erstwhile colleagues, which contrasted with the latter's more disciplined and orthodox working practices.

Balenovich et al's (2008) research into police officers working on a domestic programme therefore highlights a number of issues. First, that even quite a distinct police role (in this case, policing domestic violence) can lead to contrasting work orientations. Second, that these may be influenced by occupational factors (for example, from the police training that they receive) or biographical factors (for example, from previous employment or personal experience). Third, that particular forms of police work, such as that focusing on domestic violence, where there is a very discernible tension between the legal and the welfare-based elements of the work, are more likely to provoke ambiguous or contradictory working styles among officers. Fourth, and finally, that a variety of working orientations are apparently condoned by the culture, which might suggest that the culture of the police is less inflexible than traditional interpretations might allow. The work of Amanda Robinson (2000), among others, indicates that, traditionally, police culture tended to imbue in officers predominantly negative views towards domestic violence victims. Similarly, as we can see from earlier literature in the field of police studies, welfare elements of police work were historically viewed as 'shit' work and '... morally degrading' (Punch, 1979: 110). This point is also reinforced by Peter Manning, who noted that 'morally binding interactions are avoided or treated with disdain' (1977: 313). This can be taken to suggest that the emotional labour associated with the welfare elements of the police role sits uneasily with the masculinity that has long been associated with police institutions. However, as welfare or social work orientations to police work are increasingly becoming accepted as normal and non-gendered (see Charman, 2017), we might see a growing acceptance of cultural dispositions that view the welfare role of the police as an occupational priority.

The idea that police attitudes and values (which provide the building blocks of culture) are specifically linked to the role that police officers undertake was specifically explored by psychologists Helena Carlson and Markley Sutton (1974). Their research sought to test the extent to which psychological measures of authoritarianism (a tendency to favour order and the imposition of authority) and punitiveness (a tendency to favour harsh punishment for those who offend) would vary between different police roles. Their research was partially influenced by earlier work which suggested that high levels of either of these factors had detrimental impacts on sensitive or volatile police–public interactions. Two competing explanations, which they wanted to test, were (a) are authoritarian attitudes among police officers caused by police recruitment of individuals with high levels of authoritarianism, or (b) does the function or role that that officer undertakes determine the level of authoritarianism? Their research found that those who studied policing or police science were more likely to have punitive attitudes than non-police officers, a finding explained by the authors as being based on the need to perceive punishment as effective for a career in the criminal justice system. The more relevant results of the experiment, in respect of understanding the role played by authoritarianism and punitiveness in regard of the current theme being explored, is that the police roles most associated with high degrees of punitiveness and authoritarianism were jail aides. These members of police staff, who work in custody suites with prisoners, displayed higher levels of the trait than police academy students, patrol officers or higher-ranking officers. Indeed, the research suggests that police academy students were not particularly authoritarian in outlook, therefore providing some support for the notion that these traits were essentially linked to role rather than more individualised factors. Another interesting finding is that levels of punitiveness and authoritarianism were significantly lower among detectives and higher-ranking officers. This finding is partially explained by Carlson and Sutton (1974) as a result of the fact that those working in custody roles are spending a greater proportion of their time dealing with offenders (or suspected offenders), whereas other roles are more greatly focused on 'nonenforcement problems and interpersonal service' (1974: 63).

The cultural significance of rank

While role indeed appears to be a key determinant of the cultural outlook of officers, we should be careful not to underestimate the impact of rank. In an interesting account of how officers become socialised into the role of sergeants, John van Maanen (1984) shows how police organisations ideally seek to promote lower-ranking officers who have not been engaged predominantly on street duties. This is a conscious approach founded on the idea that a 'patrolman's mentality' (van Maanen, 1984: 157) is unsuitable for the role of police sergeant. As one of van Maanen's sample noted, 'The more you've seen outside of patrol ... the more attractive you are to the brass' (quoted in van Maanen, 1984: 159). In particular, officers felt that time spent working on administrative duties was particularly valuable to those seeking promotion. There was an exception, the case of street sergeants, who, against the odds, become promoted to sergeant from a patrol position, but such individuals were viewed very much as a minority. As a process that van Maanen perceived as excluding over 95% of those who apply, promotion was viewed as unpredictable, unfair and flawed. For those who succeed, notes van Maanen, there are five core characteristics of their socialisation into the police rank. First, for those who successfully progress through the promotion process there is often a considerable wait before they can take the promotion as they are required to wait for a suitable post to become available. While in this 'limbo', aspiring sergeants often seek postings that will minimise the likelihood of making very visible, and progress-threatening, mistakes. Risk aversion takes hold and sergeants in waiting are viewed by patrol officers as being removed from the reality of police work, an accusation that represents a strong admonishment given the central importance of 'real police work' to the cultural world of the police. And, as van Maanen shows, the values that hold such traction among the culture of street officers fail to be valued by promotion panels, meaning that new sergeants are often coldly received at their first post-promotion posting. One of the sergeants cited in van Maanen's research reflected that: 'I was here for almost six months before they started asking me for anything other than a day off. Cops are a strange breed. They don't think it's possible for someone who hasn't worked their little patch to know anything about what they do' (quoted in van Maanen, 1984: 164).

Second, van Maanen highlights how, in sharp contrast to the transition from police recruit to fully fledged police officer, the transformation from officer to sergeant is an altogether different proposition. While the former process takes place within a distinct cohort, shaped as it is by the camaraderie of the police academy, the latter is a more isolated experience as the promoted officer begins a journey away from the cultural heartland of policing towards that of police management. Whereas the act of becoming a police officer is very much a communal and supported experience, the transition to sergeant is a more solitary journey, which, if facilitated at all, is done so informally by that officer's personal and professional acquaintances.

The third core characteristic of new sergeants, according to van Maanen, is that they are unlikely to find their first posting, on promotion, to be a permanent and supervisory one. Instead, such assignments are likely to end up with sergeants of both experience and standing whose supervisory skills are already proven. New sergeants were more likely to be allocated relief assignments where they supervise different groups on each shift. To van Maanen these roles were essentially 'caretaking' roles whereby the squads being supervised would pay little heed to their regular supervisor's stand-in. To the new sergeant, therefore, it was considered important to develop professional acquaintances with those superiors who hold influence.

The fourth characteristic presented by van Maanen is the fact that, for new sergeants, their assignments are likely to be in those units which, while unlikely to be tasked with the highest priority roles, are more likely to be problematic and staffed with challenging individuals.

Such units (described as 'cow precincts' by van Maanen, 1984: 165) had a high turnover of supervisors and represented an excellent means of 'breaking in' new sergeants in environments where the sergeant's lack of experience is unlikely to be the biggest challenge faced. The final characteristic of new sergeants is that, by and large, they will find themselves working with officers who were, up to this point, unknown to them. This is important in two respects. The first is that the social and communicative shorthand that develops between acquaintances is not present. The second is that, due to their supervisory position, they are unable to witness first hand the working practices of those they supervise. A key task for new sergeants, therefore, is not only to develop relationships with new sets of colleagues but to also develop relationships of the nature that will allow the new sergeant to effectively command his or her officers.

For most sergeants, those typified by van Maanen as 'station house sergeants', the role involves a high degree of administrative knowledge and skills associated with the managerial culture of the police, a substantively removed set of values from those of the patrol officer. The degree of administration that the job entails covers data management, PR, obscure legal knowledge, multi-agency relations, cost budgeting and report and bid writing, among many others. For the other sergeants, referred to as 'street sergeants', both the role and cultural orientation are fundamentally different. For them, their responsibility lies not so much with the men they supervise but with the beat which they work. This provides a much closer cultural affiliation to the street officer than the station house sergeant as the moral foundation of their work remains the 'thin blue line' rather than the managerial oversight common to station house sergeants. Regardless of whichever orientation a sergeant belongs or subscribes to, van Maanen states, '... it is true that the administrative and street cultures of police organizations are recognized by sergeants and their men alike. Not only are they recognized, but sergeants typically perform their roles in ways more or less consistent with the dictates of one culture, and hence, opposed to the other' (1984: 170).

Van Maanen's research, while now quite dated, does provide an insight into an area that is often neglected in debates about police culture. By focusing on the socialisation processes of those officers transitioning from officer to sergeant roles we are allowed a glimpse at the intersection between role and rank and the opportunities for cultural continuity and change that exist there. Fundamentally, it appears that for the traditional sergeant, those who are undertaking a new role situated within the management sphere of police operations, the shift in rank not only represents a change in role and occupational focus but also marks a socialisation process wholly removed from the one through which they became a police officer. As noted previously, this process is essentially an individual process and one that represents anything but a seamless transition to a permanent supervisory role. Instead, it appears that the socialisation process represents a disorienting rite of passage aimed at stripping away the comfortable camaraderie that had characterised most officers' careers to date with the purpose of setting the new sergeant apart from their lower-ranking colleagues. This serves a number of reasons – to prepare the sergeant for the comparative isolation of a managerial role, to acclimatise them to the 'them and us' friction that characterises supervisor–officer relations in police organisations (see, for example, Niederhoffer, 1969; Reuss-Ianni and Ianni, 1983; Marks, 2007), and to imbue in them the skills of asserting influence over other members of their profession. Through a system of short-term supervisory relief postings, often to the more challenging areas of the organisation, those chosen for sergeant are moulded and hardened into the role. This is enacted through a loosening of their association with the lower ranks, through temporary immersion into a variety of police departments and through exposure to groups of officers who are unlikely to engage effectively with them as supervisors, regardless of the sergeant's level of skill, experience or communicative abilities.

Research undertaken by Reg Butterfield et al (2005) also explores the role of police sergeant, particularly with reference to how the role of the first level of line manager has adapted (or been adapted) to new management models within the police, not least to the introduction of techniques based on NPM (see Chapter 5). The shift away from philosophies of professionalism and administration to ideas drawn from the private and commercial sectors, the authors note, has caused an expansion in lower-level management roles within police organisations such as at the rank of sergeant. As a result, we have witnessed a distortion of the traditional 'boundaries between professional and managerial work' (2005: 331) at such levels. The challenges have been further compounded by depleted resources, resistance to reform agendas and a lack of investment in staff development in respect of these emerging roles. These recent changes have, according to Butterfield et al, seen the recasting of the police sergeant as 'practitioner-managers' (2005: 333) and, in doing so, raised potential issues about the role and focus of the police sergeant in the post-NPM police world.

As in the work of van Maanen (1984) in a US context, Butterfield et al (2005) identified that the police sergeant role incorporated a large amount of non-operational tasks in the form of managerial responsibilities. These included the use of new data systems, data management, work planning, deployment, budgetary planning and oversight, performance management and responding to public complaints. In research 'conducted in the UK' it was found that the devolution of responsibility from inspectors to sergeants did not increase autonomy or indeed power. Similarly, the increase in managerial expectation on the sergeant role to reduce the discretion of the officers they supervise led to less regular contact with their staff than previously. At the same time, the use of performance indicator regimes encouraged behaviours that ran counter to the spirit of the community policing initiatives that were in place. Likewise, the reduction in supervisor contact with officers meant that supervisors were rarely able to undertake leadership activity to rectify this. As a result of this research, Butterfield et al (2005) conclude with a number of reflections about recent changes to the role of sergeant that will enhance our understanding of police cultures. The first is that control of officer behaviour is not necessarily enhanced by expanding the managerial remit of the sergeant role. The second is that the expansion of the managerial element of the sergeant role has come to be seen as arduous and, far from reducing the administrative burden, NPM has, through the introduction of a 'target culture', unintentionally created a stifling administrative bureaucracy that reinforces non-desired behaviours. The third is that, far from replacing the police occupational culture with a more pro-management performance-oriented set of values, the traditional, and informal, cultural orientation of operational officers has become stronger.

The role of wider factors in shaping police culture

The early work of writers like Skolnick does contain the implicit suggestion that police culture is a relatively generic and universal set of embedded values operating at the level of individual police officers, and we need to be aware that an increasing amount of work does tend to work against this position. While the work of Chan (1997) has already been referred to in this book, it is appropriate here to remind ourselves of the importance of her research. Apart from advocating that a plurality of cultures exists within the police, she also draws attention to the idea that forces external to the police impact on the organisation and, as a result, its culture. While roles, therefore, are important determinants of police behaviour and values, one cannot discount the impact of other agencies within the criminal justice or security spheres on the way we structure police organisations and deliver policing. This principle can be explored by reference to, for example, the work of John Magenau and Raymond Hunt (1989), which highlights the impact of socio-political networks on police roles by suggesting that policing is influenced by social interest groups that exist in wider society. These the authors describe as the 'police agency's role-making network' (1989: 552) and can be viewed as pertaining to five different categories: 'quasi-publics', 'institutional partners', 'CJS [criminal justice system] role set', 'clientele' and 'other actors'. The first, 'quasi-publics', includes groups with an interest in police work but that fall outside the scope of the police organisation and the criminal justice system. In the UK context this might include, for example, the Police Federation of England and Wales, which represents police officers at the ranks of police constable, sergeant and inspector. The second, 'institutional partners', refers to those that have an oversight remit for the police. An example of such a role in England and Wales is that of Police and Crime Commissioners, which replaced police authorities in 2012. The third, 'CJS role set', indicates other agencies, departments and formal players in the criminal justice system. The fourth, 'clientele', is composed of members of the public and an assortment of political and lobbying groups. The fifth, 'other actors', is taken to refer to a range of localised service providers that may in some way influence the local policing environment. An example might be an individual or group of individuals who undertake police training and research within the higher education sector. Magenau and Hunt's work is important in that it shows the interplay between a variety of external forces in determining the role of the police. In particular, the role of police unionism was found to be a strong force for resisting pressure from other network actors to reduce the discretionary elements of operational policing, particularly where issues of police professionalism and the arming of the police were concerned.

While Magenau and Hunt's (1989) work draws us towards exploring the ways in which localised networks can influence the roles, function and autonomy of the police, we can also adopt a wider, or more global, focus through which to explore these issues. The work of Cynthia Enloe (1976) is particularly of interest in this respect. Writing in the area of political science she draws attention to the way in which the political elements of policing are often ignored. She attributes this to a number of factors such as the perceived localism of police operations and the fact that they are considered to be largely un-political. Her work, however, suggests that we need to be fully aware of the political dimensions of policing and the impact that this has on police work. She does this by highlighting two central themes: the militarisation of police organisations and the use of ethnic criteria in police recruitment. These, she argues, are important as they inform relationships between the police, the military and the state and furthermore influence the roles that the police undertake. Her research is important to our understanding of police culture for a number of reasons. She suggests that, even for traditional Western social democracies, such as the UK, there is an increasing trend toward the accumulation of ever more sophisticated hardware, be it arms, communication equipment or a combination of both. To Enloe this suggests an increasing tendency, globally, towards militarised models of policing. One example of this provided by Enloe (1976) is that of Malaysia, where the militarisation of the Malaysian police has led to a range of specialised policing units including a paramilitary force that is barracked, trained and tasked in a wholly different manner to the traditional police officer. As a result, her work identifies the ways in which the police role can vary considerably between national jurisdictions, blur the relationship with military institutions, reflect divergent domestic security issues and highlight different strategic views of the role of police organisations. Furthermore, Enloe shows how police recruitment targets particular ethnic groups as a means of ensuring police forces are protected against 'challenges to the existing political structure' (1976: 33). Enloe provides evidence to support these assertions when she draws on examples such as attempts to increase the recruitment of Chinese citizens into the Malaysian police, Catholics into the Royal Ulster Constabulary and more minority ethnic groups into the British police. Such measures were, partially at least, motivated by a wish to reduce internal social discord. In terms of the latter example, the ramifications of such a move would impact on police–community relations, police legitimacy among some groups and discriminatory police practices. Enloe concludes by identifying a growing tendency towards the state engaging with the three symbiotic processes of militarisation, politicisation and ethnicisation as a means of responding towards internal threats that tend to destabilise the sense of order within a given jurisdiction. The work suggests, therefore, that culture is in part impacted by factors as diverse as the relationship between the police and the military, the need of political elites to control against insurgence and the options provided by ethnic recruitment agendas for enhanced state stability. What is obvious here is that such agendas will be more or less explicit and rigorous in different national jurisdictions. An appreciation of such factors does allow, however, for a complex understanding of the different forms that police functions take, the different role they play for governments and the fact that such variations will no doubt reflect and inform cultural differences.

What this chapter has attempted to do is to provide a broad yet succinct appraisal of some of the ways we can recognise distinct differences within and between police roles, and to explore the ways in which these might be associated with different values, attitudes and work orientations. This allows us to move away from generic approaches to understanding policing towards a more complex and critical appraisal of the work of their police, their internal role differentiation and their rank structure. Such an appreciation is fundamental to understanding the ways in which police officers construct their knowledge of the highly complex social worlds, roles and organisations they operate within and, correspondingly, how they orient their own personally held values to work effectively within the more general values associated with their organisational sphere. The concept of 'cognitive burn-in' (Sklansky, 2007) is, once again, a very helpful device here as it allows police researchers to reflect on the assumptions that impact the ways in which they frame their knowledge of the police. As we have seen throughout the course of this chapter, the factors that Jerome Skolnick viewed as being integral to the police working personality (danger, authority and effectiveness) arguably apply less to the police service as a whole than to particular police roles and functions at the lower end of the rank structure. Similarly, certain components of Skolnick's model (for example, effectiveness) might vary in intensity between jurisdictions, in turn creating different dynamics within the police in particular national contexts.

What we have also seen are the challenges for quite deterministic depictions of police culture given the inherent contradictions of the police role in respect of the balance between the aims of law enforcement and public service. These present challenges of articulating the police role both at the level of strategic governance and in terms of how particular police tasks (for example, those addressing gendered crime) might provoke different working styles among officers. These might be influenced not only by a combination of the inherent tension between service and law enforcement roles but also by that officer's particular and personal history. Similarly, what are perceived as fundamental traits of the police officer personality, authoritarianism and punitiveness, seem to be much less prevalent in non-custody roles and senior ranks, leading to some intriguing directions for future police culture research among those officers working in leadership roles. This appears to be supported by some of the research that exists around the particular role of police sergeant. As we have seen in this chapter, the work of the police sergeant contrasts greatly with that of police constable, and this would suggest that there remains scope for further research exploring the extent to which this differentiation might impact at both the personal and cultural level.

Once again, therefore, we find that universal and deterministic conceptions of police culture (often based on the working lives of lower-ranking officers) fail to provide a particularly accurate articulation of policing. Indeed, the contradictions of the role, the scope for external influence and, of course, the personal history and orientation of a particular officer can lead to variations in working style and assumptions about the wider police remit. Having addressed the scope for variation and complexity within police roles, sometimes influenced by localised pressures and influences, in the following chapter we will address the impact of change in other contexts, and explore how this further complicates many of the taken-for-granted assumptions we might hold about police culture.

Questions for further consideration

1. What do you think is the most important determinant of cultural values – rank or role? Why?
2. Reflect on the different social changes, external to the police organisation, that can impact on the culture of the police.
3. What are the implications for our understanding of police culture of depicting policing as being solely about law enforcement?

Further reading

Chan, J. (1997) *Changing Police Culture: Policing in a Multicultural Society*, Cambridge: Cambridge University Press [Chapter 4].

Charman, S. (2017) *Police Socialisation, Identity and Culture*, London: Palgrave Macmillan [Chapter 6].

Sklansky, D.A. (2007) 'Seeing blue: Police reform, occupational culture, and cognitive burn-in', in M. O'Neill, M. Marks and A. Singh (eds) *Police Occupational Culture: New Debates and Directions*, New York: Elsevier, pp 19–45.

7

New contexts for police culture

A key theme throughout the book so far has been the complexity of police work and the challenge of utilising the concept of police culture in a way that reflects this. In the last two chapters, we have predominantly focused on those internal elements of policing that lead to very different working styles and orientations such as rank and role. In this chapter, we will look beyond the policing organisation to wider pressures, forces and dynamics that have, in turn, led, or are currently leading, to cultural change in the police. In doing so, once again we will draw into question the extent to which simplistic assumptions regarding police work and the communities in which it is enacted have contemporary relevance to our understanding of police culture. The chapter will begin with a brief overview of 'late modernity', a sociological concept that provides a starting point for many explanations of societal change and, indirectly, of those changes we witness in policing organisations. This will be followed by an exploration of more focused types of change agendas, which might indirectly be associated with late modernity and that link to our understanding of police culture.

Late modernity and policing

The period from the 1980s to the present day has been described, sociologically, as that of 'late modernity', and represents a substantial change in the nature of our society from the preceding era of 'modernity'. Modernity was an era characterised largely by optimism in a world based on certainty and driven by progressive values and a faith in science and technology. In this respect, it was largely a forward-looking era where challenges were perceived as being directly overcome by the application of science, technology and logic. Central to this world view was the idea of structure. This, after all, was the period of the nuclear family, further bolstered by the ordering effects of a quite robust and embedded class system. Furthermore, an array of controls (both formal and informal) were brought to bear in respect of gender. The combination of optimism and progress within the confines of an ordered and quite prescriptive society led to social stability where change and progress were present but where the pace of their evolution was quite gentle. This lies in contrast to the era that succeeded it, the late modern era. Where modernity was built on optimism and ordered structure, late modernity was founded on uncertainty and individual freedom, and these fundamental changes were bound up in broader social change at the global level. As a result, local lives were increasingly being impacted by global events, global communication and the democratisation of travel. The tightly knit communities that had provided the backbone of modernity were, in late modernity, replaced by fragmented and increasingly diverse physical communities and, simultaneously, augmented by sub-cultures rooted in new non-physical environments (for example, cyberspace). The broad post-war consensus that led to the Golden Age of policing had been replaced with a more fluid, precarious and uncertain form of lived experience that tended to exacerbate inequalities at the local and global level. Furthermore, during the period we also witnessed the emergence of what has been termed the 'Information Society'. To Haridimos Tsoukas (1997), the period of late modernity is characterised by an increasing reliance on 'knowledge', a point that is readily understandable in the light of the unparalleled expansion of information technology over recent decades. However, while the growing accessibility of data and material has been met with optimism by some commentators, Tsoukas remains quite critical of our current information-driven era. In particular, he suggests that the nature of the data we access and process nowadays is information rather than knowledge, a distinction based on the fact that knowledge is considered as being both contextualised and imbued with values. Information, instead, represents knowledge that is 'decontextualized, timeless, impersonal, value-free' (1997: 839). The importance of this distinction, suggests Tsoukas, is that, in the late modern era, the more information we have, the less we actually understand and furthermore, the more information we have, the less we trust the experts who generated that information. This is a contradiction that Tsoukas himself recognises, noting that expert knowledge is inevitably contextualised in ways that are difficult to fully understand or engage with without a degree of expertise in that subject. As a result, far from the 'Information Age' leading to greater rationality, we have witnessed greater distrust of experts and the knowledge they create, meaning that the potential benefits which that information holds is less likely to be realised. As the amount of information available to us increases, we actually witness a decrease in trust that greatly hinders the state's ability to govern rationally.

The impact of these changes can be witnessed in all aspects of modern life. However, they have been especially profound in respect of those areas for which the police hold significant responsibility – crime, fear of crime and security. To some considerable extent, this is to be expected given the significance of such issues to the concept of risk. The idea of risk, in a sociological sense, is a helpful concept through which to explore the relationship between policing, police culture and social change, and was popularised, at the conceptual level, by the author Ulrich Beck in his 1992 book *Risk Society*. Its main premise is quite straightforward in that it suggests that contemporary society is increasingly focused on the future. As a result, societies, organisations and individuals have become more intent on minimising potential risk. This relatively new way of understanding contemporary life represents a substantial departure from previous eras, when society was more accepting of risk as an inescapable aspect of existence. Simultaneous to these social processes, political systems in the West have come to increasingly reflect neoliberal values which, according to David Harvey (2007: 2), are characterised by 'strong private property rights, free markets, and free trade'.

Neoliberalism opposes extensive public spending within state institutions such as the police and, in the process, tends to work towards a narrowing of the focus of the state's remit. When policing is reconfigured to meet the needs of the neoliberal agenda, notes Jeremy Kaplan-Lyman (2012) in his essay on neoliberal policing in New York City, it is done in a way that neglects the need to do so in a context that positively engages with the public and that pays sufficient attention to accountability and governance. In conclusion, he suggests that these all hold potentially negative impacts for the legitimacy of the police. Moreover, the challenges associated with late modernity such as fragmentation or disembeddedness of experience, a focus on risk and a related anxiety or fear of crime are exacerbated by the neoliberal context. This creates a fundamental issue of supply and demand in respect of the state's ability or obligation to satisfy the public's need for security. In the risk society, disparate insecurities around a wide range of concerns become entwined with those risk-based anxieties surrounding crime (see Walklate and Mythen, 2008) to create a seemingly intractable and emotive sense of fear of crime. At the same time, while the public demand for security increases as a result of such processes, increasingly the state is less likely to have the resources (or, it has to be said, the political will) to respond.

This changing social context is incredibly important for our understanding of contemporary policing, a fact recognised by Eugene McLaughlin in his book *The New Policing* (2007). Since the 1990s, he suggests, police scholars have recognised that such changes have had a substantial impact on our understanding of police work. He states that 'the starting point for any contemporary analysis of policing must be the recognition that economic and cultural globalization, dematerialization of production processes, new information and telecommunication technologies and networks, commodification and mass consumerism, and profound and rapid social complexity have all worked to alter the institutional configuration of Western society' (McLaughlin, 2007: 87).

The ambiguity, instability and insecurity which, as a result of the processes of late modernity, characterise our modern world necessitate, according to McLaughlin, a re-evaluation of the ways in which we strategise and operationalise police work. Furthermore, the drift into late modernity mirrored the advent of high-crime societies (see Garland, 2001), signalling a growing normalisation of crime. Crime, as a result, became something to manage rather than to eradicate, and members of the public began to see crime as a common, if not attractive, facet of everyday life. Against the background of a retreating state, insecurity (as crime does) becomes normalised, and this leads to the public becoming increasingly likely to question the legitimacy of the police (Terpstra and van der Vijver, 2006).

This backdrop of economic, political and social change requires us to revisit the issue of police culture and the relevance it has in the late modern society. If we look back to the origins of academic interest in police culture, it is worth noting that police culture is very much a concept associated with the period of modernity. In other words, it was developed prior to the advent of late modernity. Furthermore, traditional ideas regarding the nature of police culture very much reflected modernist values of structure and logic, and this was demonstrated, to give but one example, by the somewhat deterministic assumptions that underpinned our thinking about the relationship between police values and behaviour. Police culture was seen as an easily definable set of values that were generally viewed as common to all officers. The social and societal changes that we have witnessed since the 1980s have not so much lessened the validity of the concept of police culture as made us more aware of the variety of ways in which the concept can be used. Commonly, our interest in police culture appeared to very much focus at the micro level of police interaction with the public and, while this is still an area of concern for academics (see, for example, the work of Long and Joseph-Salisbury, 2019), it is also true to say that we have seen a renewed interest in the relationship between policing and more abstract and externally driven agendas. Two such agendas that will provide the focus for the remainder of this chapter are the issues of police professionalisation and police ethics.

The professionalisation agenda

One response to the changing social context that has impacted on policing so markedly has been the growing prevalence of reform processes that seek to professionalise the occupation. Professionalisation is a broad term and one that deserves a certain degree of clarification. David Sklansky (2014), for example, identifies four different approaches to understanding police professionalism. The first is where professionalism is seen as a way of increasing the quality of the professional practice engaged in by officers. The second is where professionalism refers to the ways in which occupations increase their status (to that of profession) and thereafter seek autonomy as a means of resisting interference at a political level. The third is where professionalism is used to articulate that occupational practice draws not on experiential knowledge but on a legitimate, established and tested knowledge base. That is, that there exists a body of credible professional knowledge that informs practice. The final approach to understanding professionalism, according to Sklansky, is to view it as a process whereby practitioners act in appropriate ways, not because of the influence and control of external bodies but because they have internalised professional norms. Despite this attempt to explain the various conceptions of professionalism, Sklansky admits that these individual elements are intricately connected.

The concept of professionalism is a challenging area, not least because we tend to differentiate it in respect of whether we are applying it to 'old' or 'new' professions. The work of two writers, Julia Evetts (2013) and Valerie Fournier (1999), in particular, help us to explain this distinction by exploring the fundamental differences between professionalism in these two contexts (see Cockcroft, 2015). Essentially the distinction rests on the idea that for 'new' professions (for example, policing, nursing and social work), professionalisation, rather than a process whereby an occupation is granted autonomy, refers to the application of 'disciplinary logic' (Fournier, 1999: 288). Similarly, Evetts (2013) suggests that new professions (as opposed to the 'old' professions connected to legal work and the higher levels of the medical profession) are controlled not from within but from above. In other words, the 'new' professions enjoy none of the autonomy of the 'old' professions. This can be explained, according to Fournier (1999), as ultimately being caused by late modernity. She argues that the changes that are associated with late modernity have meant that, for some occupations, work has become increasingly unstructured and hard to control. The resulting 'disciplinary gap' (Fournier, 1999: 281) is filled by a model of professionalisation which is largely synonymous with the idea of regulation. Furthermore, the rise of 'new' professions appears to have been motivated in many cases by a desire to reduce the opportunities for discretionary work practices in public sector occupations (Cockcroft, 2015). This potentially positions 'new' professionalism agendas in policing as attempts to limit or restrain the impact of police cultures on police behaviour.

It is relevant here to refer to one of the major challenges posed by professionalisation for policing and its culture, its impact on discretion. As noted previously, discretion is an integral element of the police culture, and one that, arguably, has commanded insufficient explicit scrutiny from academics, police leaders and policy makers alike. While much work has been undertaken to address what are viewed as the manifestations of police culture, such as discriminatory behaviours, comparatively little focus has been given to that part of the police role that allows such problematic manifestations of the culture to occur. At one level of analysis, discretion represents the key to understanding police culture. This is because discretion is both an essential part of the police role and, simultaneously, one of the most symbolically important and valued elements of the police culture. To add a further layer of complexity, discretion is viewed by the police leadership as perhaps the key factor that is common to elements of police practice that they view as unprofessional and/or inappropriate. It also therefore represents a dilemma in respect of the delivery of good police practice as it is an essential, and integral, element of the police role. At the same time, however, it can lead to both appropriate and inappropriate police practice, and is viewed by many police officers as pivotal to their perceptions of both personal professionalism and the professionalism of the occupation of as a whole.

Contemporary attempts to address police professionalism through police reforms are, it can be argued, consistently founded on ideas that seek to limit police discretion. As we can see above from the work of Evetts (2013) and Fournier (1999), the professionalisation of public sector occupations are often driven by perceived needs to introduce a greater element of control over the working lives of practitioners in these fields. Where policing is concerned, the reduction of police officer discretion is a key area where such control can be exerted. However, such approaches bring a number of challenges for police practice. First, it is difficult to envisage ways in which police discretion can be limited given the wide remit of the police role, the reactive nature of the work and the status of the police as the service that deals with those occurrences that fall beyond the responsibility of other agencies (Cockcroft, 2017). Second, as noted by Mike Brogden (1982), the legislation that represents the legal tools that are used by officers is often very much reliant on the notion of police discretion. Finally, the idea of restricting police culture as a means of encouraging greater professionalism has serious ramifications, somewhat ironically, for the sense of professional worth among officers given that discretion has not only a very real practical value, but also a symbolic value for officers.

In terms of the first of these, the practical element, it is not hard to envisage the benefits of discretion. The scope of police work is so broad that the ability to make professionally informed judgements is of central value to officers. It allows them to draw on their professional experience, and that of their colleagues, to make decisions that represent the best possible outcome given the restrictions of their role and their powers combined with the particular characteristics of the situation that they are in. Furthermore, it is difficult to envisage how a police organisation without such discretional powers would operate within the real world. Officers will undoubtedly and inevitably face challenges in their working lives, where discretionary 'freedom' is required to fashion a response to situations they never expected or were trained to face.

There is, therefore, substantial evidence to suggest that much of the motivation to embark on a professionalisation agenda is consistent with the first of Sklansky's categories, where professionalism is associated with an increase in the quality of work undertaken by practitioners. Evidence can be found for this in the College of Policing's *Leadership Review* of 2015. While advocating a rethinking of how the police engage with the idea of leadership, it also strongly proposed a vision of a fully professional police service. The document itself repeatedly draws on the language and rhetoric of professionalism. For example:

> Leadership is a primary issue for a body establishing the elements of a formal profession. It sits at the heart of what it means to practise as a professional and it is the responsibility of a professional body to state what can be expected of leaders in that profession. (2015: 7)

> Adopting elements that can be associated with its development as a profession can help policing assure the quality of its service in a changing context. (2015: 18)

> Policing at its best is based on knowledge allied to professional judgement, not on hierarchy wedded to procedure and process. (2015: 18)

While there can be no doubt that raising the quality of police work to meet the changing societal context of the contemporary world is a key driver of the professionalisation agenda, it is possible to identify other factors. A strong case can also be made to support the idea that the professionalisation agenda is very much a result of the fact that, since the 1960s, the British public have placed less trust in the police. As police legitimacy has therefore declined it has been possible to identify what P.A.J. Waddington (1998) termed a 'crisis in policing'. Reform brings a wide variety of benefits, not all of which are connected to practitioner performance, one of which, for example, is the opportunity to enhance the public view of policing by invoking the somewhat nebulous concept of professionalisation. Furthermore, Katja Hallenberg and myself (2017) chart some of these broader externally facing benefits. By identifying itself as a profession (rather than an occupation), policing promotes itself as an authority on those subject areas aligned to its role. By becoming credible authorities in this way, Sklansky (2014) suggests that the police become perceived as being more efficient in their work. Similarly, where police professionalisation agendas are achieved through partnership with higher education institutions, further benefits accrue such as, for example, better quality police–public relationships, improved relationships with both the government and other professions, and a greater ability to counter negative judgements of police competence (Hallenberg, 2012). A common feature of many of these claims is that the benefits for the police of professionalisation are largely symbolic and external-facing rather than directly related to the improved professionalism and competency of officers (Hallenberg and Cockcroft, 2017). In our research, which studied police officers who had undertaken higher education programmes while serving as police officers, we found some interesting tensions around the relationship between higher education and professionalisation. Whereas police organisations often supported officers both in terms of the financial burden of studying and in terms of protecting learning time, on completion many felt that no value was placed on their achievements by their employing organisation. Moreover, officers felt that their engagement with higher education was also met with some cultural resistance from both their peers and from senior officers. For example, one sergeant interviewed for the research recalled:

> There was a guy came in he had a PhD apparently and on his email signature it sort of said you know –PC452ST, PhD at the end of it. And apparently his sergeant said to him "take that off you XXXX that means nothing." And there is still very much a culture of a degree is something that you ought to hide. (quoted in Hallenberg and Cockcroft, 2017: 281)

The relationship between professionalisation and higher education, therefore, is complex. It has been well documented by earlier research that the pragmatism of the police culture has meant that officers were disparaging of higher education and those who engaged with it. At the same time, much of the academic writing about policing has been largely critical of police practice. It is probably fair to suggest, therefore, that for many years policing and academia occupied separate, distinct and often mutually antagonistic worlds. Recent years, however, have seen a much greater sense of partnership between the two (see, for example, Goode and Lumsden, 2018), and this has led to significant numbers of mutually beneficial collaborations. However, while the previous degree of mutual antagonism may have dissipated, there remains a cultural challenge in respect of the extent to which the values of academia should permeate police practice.

One area where this cultural division becomes acutely noticeable is in the rise of the EBP agenda and the way in which this has brought to the fore arguments about the respective roles that evidential and experiential knowledge should have in the police world. In particular, a sizeable question has arisen in respect of what actually constitutes knowledge in policing. And, while this may not seem to bear much relation to the subject of police culture, on closer inspection we can see how it becomes apparent that police culture is, in fact, central to this argument. As we have seen from earlier chapters, EBP has become incredibly influential as a preferred model through which we should generate knowledge about policing. By adopting the rigour of the empirical sciences to establish what works and what does not work in policing we can create, proponents suggest, a knowledge base which, while informally bolstering the professional status of the police, will, in parallel, raise the quality of the work that police undertake. However, the aforementioned pragmatism of the police culture can be seen, in many respects, as strongly opposed to the concept of EBP. This is because police officers have traditionally recognised the value of experiential knowledge, informal knowledge with no basis in scientific testing that nevertheless proves useful to the police in supporting them in their duties (Williams and Cockcroft, 2019).

To fully understand the resistance of some officers to EBP, it is necessary to explore the issue of police knowledge in a little more depth. The work of Dominic Wood et al (2017) begins by acknowledging the benefits of EBP, most notably in respect of its timely acknowledgement that the role of police knowledge is an important area that has been largely neglected. Likewise, they suggest that it also allows for the inherent authority of the rank structure to be challenged in relation to what is considered appropriate knowledge. In other words, EBP advocates an abstract body of knowledge that derives its authority not from the rank of the officer presenting or using that knowledge but through the scientific rigour of the method by which that knowledge was created. At the same time, Wood et al (2017) do forward some concerns with EBP and its associated professionalisation agenda. In particular, they raise issue with what they see as a quite narrow methodological focus and a lack of context. The first of these refers to the preferred methodological approach of the randomised controlled trial (RCT), a scientific approach to generating data and, subsequently, knowledge. The RCT is a popular means of testing the effectiveness of one intervention over another by simply exploring the impact of the new intervention (for example, a new form of community policing) in comparison to a control group (for example, an old form of community policing). By doing so, it is believed that this comparison allows us to chart the effectiveness of the 'new' way of undertaking whatever phenomenon it is we are investigating. This method is tremendously popular within the sphere of health and medicine where it allows us to explore the effectiveness of, for example, a new asthma treatment by comparing the experiences and physiological reaction of one group of asthma sufferers treated with the established treatment with another group who undertake the new treatment.

However, the application of this approach to establishing the effectiveness of interventions (or, to put it another way, new ways of responding to problems) has been criticised, not on the grounds of the validity of the method but on its application to the complexities of policing. Clinical trials of, for example, new drugs and treatments take place against a sterile and controlled clinical backdrop. Policing takes place against a very different set of conditions and it has been argued, by Wood et al (2017), that RCTs fail to reflect, or adequately account for, the different social, political and cultural contexts within which it occurs. In short, therefore, it is difficult to appreciate the relevance and applicability of RCT results without fully understanding the nuances of the conditions through which they were created. The same issue persists when applying that knowledge to different contexts, with the argument being that there needs to be contextual similarity for the findings to remain relevant and appropriate. Other issues may also be identified, such as those surrounding the extent to which existing knowledge remains appropriate as police objectives and practices change. Likewise, given the importance of personal and professional reflection to the practice of policing (see College of Policing, no date), it is difficult to see how this can be reconciled with the abstract and hard knowledge that is often associated with EBP.

At a more cultural level, this does make us question what forms of knowledge and skills constitute police work, with some academics (see, for example, Tong et al, 2009) viewing it as a combination of science, craft and art. Martin Innes (2010: 32, cited in Wood et al, 2017) goes so far as to suggest that, 'effective policing is more "art" or "craft" than "science"', and, if correct, this creates certain challenges for the implementation of EBP. To fully appreciate such issues, however, it may be helpful to draw on the work of Michael Eraut (2000, cited in Williams and Cockcroft, 2019), who differentiated between 'personal' and 'codified' knowledge, where 'personal' knowledge is associated with informal, cultural or tacit knowledge and 'codified' knowledge is that which is formalised, structured and usually disseminated from above. EBP represents therefore a type of codified knowledge that is largely generated without the input of lower-level practitioners. Personal knowledge, however, would, in terms of a policing context, be more associated with that which is generated and transmitted at a cultural level between practitioners. A helpful example we might use to illustrate this comes from Brogden et al (1988), who described the relationship between police knowledge, police discretion and police culture in the following way: 'the occupational subculture equips them with the knowledge of how to deal with their substantial (legally granted) discretion on a day-to-day basis. And management initiatives to control the rank and file officer continually have to contend with this legally sanctioned discretion and the "space" it offers the occupational subculture' (1988: 35). While it is appropriate to be aware of the potential that such 'space' has to lead to unprofessional practice, it is also necessary to appreciate the need for cultural and contextual knowledge as a means of making 'codified' knowledge relevant. An example of this can be drawn from my work with colleagues (Cockcroft et al, 2018), which explored the challenges of developing effective cybercrime training programmes for police officers. We found that cybercrime presents real challenges for many officers as they may struggle to understand both the technology that underpins such offences and the ways in which they would incorporate the formal knowledge they have about cybercrime into their working role. Through survey research we found that, while 'formalised' knowledge has a substantial role in some elements of their learning, police officers very much benefit from group-based learning opportunities that give them the opportunity to discuss contextual issues around how such abstract knowledge would be applied in real-life situations. Much like our understanding of how officers use discretion to understand how legal knowledge is applied in practice, so, too, it appears that a similar process is involved in the assimilation of technical knowledge. Therefore, while abstract knowledge is important to police work, cultural assimilation, made possible by informal peer interaction, has a crucial part to play in giving police officers an understanding of how to apply the knowledge they have learned. Such findings appear to support the work of Richard Heslop (2011), who states that police learning is a distinct social and cultural process rather than a passive one. Furthermore, the importance of socially and culturally derived knowledge is highlighted by the work of Dale Ballucci et al (2017), who explored police officer reactions to the introduction of case management risk tools in intimate partner violence (IPV) situations. These risk tools, based on formalised research-based knowledge, were met with some opposition from officers as they believed such formalised mechanisms devalued the informal cultural knowledge and skills that police used in such cases. Officers tended to place much more value on experiential knowledge, of both investigation and IPV, which officers gain from doing the job and from working with other officers, rather than the abstract formal knowledge derived from the risk assessment tools. Another allied concern was that such tools limited the scope for experientially informed discretionary decision-making. As we can see from these examples, culturally derived knowledge has real-world utility in helping officers to understand the relevance of abstract formal knowledge to their day-to-day roles. At the same time, cultural knowledge has also become, like discretion, an important and much coveted symbol of the professionalism of the police occupation.

Ethics

In July 2014, the College of Policing launched its *Code of Ethics* for police officers in England and Wales, with the stated aim of supporting 'each member of the police profession to deliver the highest professional standards in their service to the public' (2014: iv). The document outlines a set of principles and standards of professional behaviour and guidance on how breaches of the Code will be managed within police organisations. The principles proposed under the Code are Accountability, Fairness, Honesty, Integrity, Leadership, Objectivity, Openness, Respect and Selflessness, and their stated intent was to influence individual police values and behaviour and to direct the organisational culture of the police (College of Policing, 2014). The standards of behaviour identified by the *Code of Ethics* were Honesty and Integrity, Authority, Respect and Courtesy, Equality and Diversity, Use of Force, Orders and Instructions, Duties and Responsibilities, Confidentiality, Fitness for Work, Conduct and Challenging and Reporting Improper Behaviour. These, the document states, represent the expected standards of police practice held by both the College of Policing and the public.

While at one level this initiative represents another strand in the professionalisation agenda, it should also be noted that ethics in policing can also be understood at a more removed level. This is illustrated by Peter Neyroud, who suggested that 'Police ethics includes both the values that underpin professional and democratic policing together with the moral decisions faced by police officers at all levels of the organization in the course of their work and the basis on which these are resolved' (2008: 97). Neyroud continues by identifying three key interrelated elements of police ethics around which discussion has arisen: styles of policing, the police institution and police organisational culture. It is seen that particular styles of policing, such as crime fighting, are more likely to lead to ethical challenges than others. Where there is such an organisational focus that favours law enforcement over community policing initiatives, we are more likely to see the police engaging in morally and professionally questionable practices (for example, noble cause corruption) due to the pressure for results. This form of professional malpractice results not from the motivation of individual gain but from organisational pressure, leading to officers having to engage in inappropriate practice to achieve the appropriate legitimate ends. This example, in particular, highlights the ethical interplay between the moral elements of decision-making at the individual level and the higher-level organisational goals of the police institution in respect of, in this case, crime control. Ethical policing can therefore be considered to have its roots not just in the moral outlook of individual officers but also in the way in which institutional pressure is brought to bear in ways that make it difficult to police ethically. The role of police culture in the debate surrounding police ethics has generally focused on the assumption that informal values and assumptions work against the adoption of ethical policing behaviours.

To explore these issues in a little greater depth it is helpful to draw on the work of Louise Westmarland (2005) and Louise Westmarland and Michael Rowe (2018). The first of these pieces of research reports on questionnaire research carried out with police officers to explore their attitudes to a range of unethical behaviours. Its findings are interesting in that they suggest that officers have a considerable understanding of the ethical requirements placed on them and of issues of professional integrity. Furthermore, officers also differentiate between different forms of unethical behaviour. For example, they are more likely to view acquisitive crime (that is, police crime that leads to some monetary reward for the individual) as unacceptable regardless of the value of benefit to be had and, correspondingly, they are more likely to report such behaviour to superiors. At the same time, those acts which involve the use of excessive force against members of the public or which involve the 'bending' of the law were viewed with less concern and were less likely to be reported. In conclusion, Westmarland highlights the importance of police culture to any debate over police ethics because of the influence of the culture in inhibiting the reporting of unethical behaviours through formal mechanisms. In a piece of follow-up research, published in 2018, Westmarland and Rowe develop many of the arguments originally presented in their earlier work, and again found that police officers considered those unethical behaviours that resulted in personal gain for the officer to be the most serious, and were therefore more likely to be reported. Other patterns of interest were also identified. For example, there was little difference in results based on the respondent's gender, suggesting that male and female officers held similar views about what constituted unethical policing and which types of behaviour were most appropriate to report. However, an important finding emerges here regarding differences in attitudes between officers working in rural and urban areas. The cultural differences between rural and urban police officers have been reported earlier in this book (see, for example, Terpstra, 2017), and it appears that these differences extend to perceptions of unethical behaviour. Rural officers were significantly more likely to report unethical behaviour and were more likely to view minor misdemeanours as unacceptable. One explanation forwarded for this by the authors was the tendency for rural communities to have more tightly knit police communities and for poor police practice in such areas to have a significantly greater impact on a police officer's career and, finally, that in such environments the public were much more likely to become aware of such behaviours. Further findings reported in Westmarland and Rowe's paper were that officers in supervisory roles were significantly more likely to report unethical behaviours than those working in non-supervisory roles. Likewise, length of police service was also seen as exerting influence on the formal reporting of unethical police behaviours, with officers with less than five years of service being less likely to report it and officers with more than 15 years' service being more likely to report it. As with Westmarland's (2005) paper, the authors found that there was a significant issue here in respect of police culture, which was evidenced by the fact that officers knew when a particular behaviour was unethical but often failed to formally report it.

The above findings are interesting in that they can be taken as evidence to reinforce the idea that, assuming culture is an impediment to ethical policing, it is particularly an issue of concern for those officers in the lower ranks, for those of limited length of service and for those working in urban policing environments. These tend to support the traditional ideas that we have around police culture, particularly in respect of it negatively impacting the work of those officers undertaking operational work in high-population communities with complex social characteristics. While at one level such research findings are helpful, it is also worth considering the extent to which ethical issues impact in other policing roles – for example, for officers working in child protection, terrorism and, indeed, senior leadership.

Two aspects of police ethics that relate to police culture and that should be considered at this point are made clear in a paper by Lawrence Sherman (1982). Despite being written over 30 years ago, this paper highlights the changing balance between police ethical awareness and the traditional cultural values of the police and the challenges for ethical police work caused by complexities particular to the police role. The traditional values held by officers, according to Sherman (1982), suggest that police actions are often determined by non-legal factors such as the characteristics of the suspect and whether individuals show respect for authority. Furthermore, he states that officers also considered the use of physical force and deception to be informal tools of the occupation, had a disregard for due process, were dismissive of 'social-work problems' (1982: 15), saw the accepting of gifts from the public (under some circumstances) as permissible and finally, viewed loyalty to colleagues as a priority. Sherman (1982) acknowledges that these values have certainly become less prevalent or intense over recent years as a result of a number of factors including the growing diversity of police recruits (in respect of ethnicity, gender and educational status), the growing focus of the media on police behaviour and the increasingly uncompromising approach of police organisations in dealing with the transgressions of their officers. Similarly, Sherman notes in respect of the US context that traditional modes of operational policing (based on the values described above) have died out as a result of both their negative impact on community relations and the rise of litigation against police departments. That said, while some of the excesses of the latter end of the 20th century may arguably have been curbed, the #BlackLivesMatter movement reminds us of the seemingly intractable nature of many of these ethical challenges.

When we turn to the second issue, the complex ethical challenges associated with the police world, Sherman again provides some valuable insights. To Sherman (1982), many of the ethical dimensions of police work are quite straightforward. For example, he notes that it would be difficult to defend any police officer engaged in the behaviour of theft. However, he continues by noting that there exist many areas where the particular characteristics of the police role would lead to the emergence of much more complex and difficult-to-resolve police ethical dilemmas. In particular, Sherman refers here to police use of force, the constraints of time, the presence of discretion and the impact of loyalty. We have already addressed, earlier in the book, the challenges and responsibilities that come with the appropriate exercise of police discretion. Decisions about what constitutes an appropriate degree of force may be influenced by the degree of perceived harm the recipient offers to both the officer and the public, and these decisions are often made in real time and without the benefit of objective information. Indeed, it is not difficult to understand that, in the heat of a particular situation, and with very little information to hand, officers might make decisions that, with the benefit of hindsight, they might regret. Similarly, it is not difficult to understand how loyalty may serve to cloud judgement in an organisation where the inherent camaraderie of the culture can lead to both personal loyalty based on friendship and more transactional forms of loyalty based on the rank structure. Furthermore, an added layer of complexity becomes apparent in respect of what Iain Densten (1999: 46) refers to as the 'paradox of accountability'. This concept, simply put, suggests that, while police officers are personally accountable for their decisions and behaviours, the breadth of the police role means that, for many situations, it is difficult, if not impossible, to know what constitutes a 'good' decision or outcome.

For Sherman, one of the key challenges here is about how we socialise police officers into thinking ethically. While he acknowledges the advances to police training and education that have been put in place over recent years, he perceives that, as far back as the 1980s, police ethics training relied too much on 'war stories', anecdotes from more experienced police officers that tended to reinforce an ethical position closely aligned to the values of the culture rather than to 'legal and societal values' (1982: 16). Through this process it is quite straightforward to understand how this becomes an important element in the cultural reproduction of the police organisation. This also appears to be reinforced by the practical advice offered to new police recruits when they leave the classroom and embark on their first experiences of street police work. Using two quotations, the first from a London police officer who served in the Metropolitan Police Service between the 1930s and the 1950s and the second cited in Sherman's work, we can see a consistent disparagement of 'formal' learning:

> But, of course, most of the Sergeants were ... well I would say ... not very educated ... you used to take a report in and they would look at it and they'd cross things out.... So you'd say, "Well ... what's that for?" They'd say, "Well ... you don't want that ... you don't want that".... You'd say, "Well, that's what you're taught at Peel House".... Then they'd say, "Forget all you learned in Peel House [the former training school for the Metropolitan Police Service]. This is how you make a report". (police officer, quoted in Cockcroft, 2001: 105)

> Forget everything they taught you in the academy, kid; I'll show you how police work is really done. (police officer, quoted in Sherman, 1982: 13)

At this point a tension emerges. Earlier in the chapter a case was made to suggest that there is substantial value to the experiential elements of police learning as it allows officers to fully understand the ways in which formal knowledge can be made applicable to real-life situations. However, there is a case to suggest that ethical knowledge in policing may be most effectively transmitted through a more abstract method of learning delivery. This certainly appears to be the preference of Sherman (1982), who suggests that such an approach holds a number of benefits. First, it allows officers to reflect on these dilemmas in a more constructive way, away from the immediacy of a given situation. Second, it allows these ethical issues to be worked through away from the peer pressure exerted by colleagues. Third, and finally, such issues also need to be reflected on away from the hierarchical pressures that can be exercised by line managers and other supervisors. In short, therefore, Sherman appears to advocate police officers having ethical knowledge prior to entering the police field.

The College of Policing's *Code of Ethics* tends to mirror this concern for a more abstract reading of police ethics, drawing as it does on the Committee on Standards in Public Life's *Principles of Public Life*. Westmarland and Rowe's (2018) research has relevance here as it provides some speculation on the likely success of the Code in the light of the findings generated by their research. In particular, they draw attention to the requirement, under the Code, for officers to formally report the behaviour of colleagues that fails to meet the expected requirements. This provides a substantial testing ground through which to assess the resilience of the culture in the face of such a new strategic initiative. At the same time, the authors note, the fact that there is considerable ambiguity (and a lack of guidance) surrounding what is and what is not inappropriate police behaviour may provide some challenges as the Code is embedded into routine practice.

In conclusion, this chapter has directed our focus away from those elements of the police role that influence the cultural world of the police to those wider forces that can be situated in the external world. Some of these, like the social change associated with late modernity, are more abstract and intangible. However, others, such as the professionalisation agenda and the associated idea of ethical policing, are more directly tied to contemporary political agendas surrounding the role of the public sector and the standards of conduct we expect from people who work in it. Central to these issues are shifting values surrounding whether the police constitute an occupation or a profession and, if it is a profession, the extent to which it should operate with relative autonomy from external forms of interference and regulation. Such matters inescapably draw us back to the concept of discretion, the notion that officers invariably possess a substantial degree of unsupervised freedom over the choices they make. Many of the tensions that we can identify surrounding the professionalisation agenda relate to a cultural battle over this concept, and advocates for police reform seek to limit, control or make more transparent the use of police operational discretion.

Questions for further consideration

1. To what extent does rapid social change work against the idea of a strong and coherent police culture?
2. Reflect on the argument that police organisations need to become more professional. What kind of changes do you think are needed? Why?

3. What are the advantages and disadvantages of the introduction of the *Code of Ethics* for police officers?

Further reading

Cockcroft, T. (2013) *Police Culture: Themes and Concepts*, London: Routledge [Chapter 4].

College of Policing (2014) *Code of Ethics: A Code of Practice for the Principles and Standards of Professional Behaviour for the Policing Profession of England and Wales*, London: College of Policing.

Westmarland, L. and Rowe, M. (2018) 'Police ethics and integrity: Can a new code overturn the blue code?', *Policing and Society*, 28(7): 854–70.

8

Conclusion

This book has attempted to explore, in a meaningful way, the somewhat idiosyncratic concept of police culture. Like any other form of culture, it is abstract, intangible and non-physical, yet impacts greatly across a wide range of subjects in a variety of ways. Increasingly, it has begun to attract attention not just from academics (who have found themselves drawn to the subject since the latter part of the 20th century) but also from those professional bodies that will shape the form of policing for years to come. Given the increasing sense of partnership between the higher education sector and the police institution, the impact of the PEQF and the continued debate about police professionalisation, it is my hope that this book will be of some support to a range of people, across academia and police organisations, who want to understand both the established and the emergent themes in this area.

As mentioned in the Introduction (Chapter 1), the book has attempted to avoid, where possible, the normative or reformist stance that some authors adopt when tackling such issues. This is for a number of reasons. First and foremost, the book has tried to avoid adopting an overly politicised voice that invariably rests on structural assumptions that might distract us from the matter at hand. Second, I believe that, quite simply, such 'critical' approaches limit our ability to adequately explain all of the issues we are dealing with here. Instead, the focus has largely been on the issue of policing's relationship with change. As our world continues its trajectory through late modernity we are experiencing an array of changing social dynamics and forces, all of which, in some way, impact on the structural and cultural elements of the police. The result is a subject area where history weighs heavily on its present despite the substantial changes it has been subjected to. As a result, a thematic approach has been adopted which provides a specific focus for the chapters while also allowing for synergies between these themes to become explicit. At the same time, the book has attempted, as far as one can with a slippery subject like culture, to present it in a way that helps police officers to identify the importance of culture, and its associated ideas, to their occupational world and, in many ways, to the strategic direction of police organisations more generally.

The book began with an exploration of what we mean by 'police culture'. As intimated above, culture, in any of its forms, remains a challenging idea, not least in respect of its non-physical nature. Police culture enjoys further definitional complexities as one realises that the term has, for much, if not all, of its existence, had a certain political or politicised element. The fact that it has largely become synonymous with poor police practice, to many commentators from both the academic and policy worlds, means that definitions can be prone to subjective or political bias. This theme was extended in Chapter 3, where the contribution of different academic disciplines to our knowledge of police culture was identified. Over time, sociological, historical, socio-legal and psychological research have all contributed to our understanding of policing and the way it shapes and influences the assumptions, values and attitudes of police officers. While much of this research has not directly set out to extend our knowledge of police culture, it has nevertheless provided knowledge that can be used to develop the concept. Other forms of research aim to have a more direct impact. EBP, for example, seeks not so much to further our understanding of police culture, but to provide an alternative knowledge base to that which informs a substantial degree of police practice. In doing so, it reminds us that all forms of knowledge are driven by different agendas and assumptions. Far from detracting from the matter at hand, however, this allows for the subject area of police culture to remain a vibrant area of debate and discussion for practitioners and academics alike.

The book then addressed the relationship between police culture and operational policing, by reference to the manifestations of police culture identified through much of the earlier research in this subject area. In doing so, it charts the somewhat deterministic models that have found support over recent years, before drawing attention to more contemporary research in the area that identifies new ways of understanding the relationship between police culture and operational policing. As a result, it should encourage readers to be critical and questioning of the concept of police culture and the ways in which it impacts on the reality of police work. From a focus on operational policing (the traditional focus for attention in police culture), the book then explored the relationship between police culture and leadership, and addressed the idea that there exist cultural tensions between leadership and operational police cultures. Similarly, it charted the substantial impact of NPM (itself driven by wider social change associated with neoliberalism) and the ways in which this has influenced the professionalisation agenda.

Our focus then turned to the relationship between police roles and police culture, and the fact that police organisations tend to be incredibly broad in respect of the number of roles they take responsibility for. The argument arises here, therefore, that the cultural dynamics of police work are largely dependent on, and driven by, the particular role that an officer undertakes. In considering culture in this way, we challenge more generic models of police assumptions, values and behaviours, and propose that a plurality of cultural adaptations to police working environments exists. From such matters of internal differentiation, the book then turned its attention to the ways in which external contexts can impact on police culture. Here, the book identified two key examples, the macro forces associated with late modernity and the more micro influences of the police professionalisation and ethics agendas, to identify the ways in which the outside world can, intentionally or otherwise, impact on the culture of the police. In this way, the book looked to promote a fluid rather than a static understanding of police culture, where the culture responds to shifting influences from beyond its own immediate operational sphere.

The final section of this chapter will serve as a focus for reflection, particularly for those who work in police organisations. It will do so in two main ways. First, it will invite the reader to reflect on the relevance of the concept of police culture. This is important, as more recent work in the area has tended to be substantially different in focus and form to earlier works and been quite critical of many earlier assumptions. Second, it will propose that the relationship between professionalisation, discretion and ethics provides ample scope to reflect on the responsibilities and obligations of police officers in the modern police, not least in respect of the balance between prescriptive standards and the informal obligations to fellow officers and colleagues. Finally, it will make a brief case to consider the relationship between police cultures and communities of practice. It will therefore revisit a number of key thematic areas that will serve as prompts for police practitioners to reflect on where police culture impacts on their professional practice, and also serve as areas of discussion and debate for those studying or researching policing. In the preceding chapters we have looked at many ideas concerning police culture or that are in some way related to it. As a result, many areas have been covered that address a range of ideas spanning the nature of academia (for example, ways in which different academic disciplines set out to research and generate meaningful knowledge about policing), social change (for example, the impact of late modernity on police work), operational police work (for example, the nature of police–public interaction) and policy (for example, the professionalisation agenda). Some of these might appear more relevant to the day-to-day professional practice of serving police officers than others. However, as this book has hopefully succeeded in conveying, while the study of police culture draws our attention to a wide variety of subject areas, it is often difficult to isolate one such area and understand it without the context provided by those other areas. To understand, for example, the challenges of gendered and racialised police practice, we need to understand the basis by which our knowledge of this subject has been generated, the wider social context of prejudice, the role that discretion has in allowing such prejudices to transform from personally held values into behaviours and finally, the ways in which complex policing institutions respond to such behaviours. In other words, to comprehend police culture one needs to appreciate a broad range of different areas of knowledge, and it is hoped that the preceding chapters have provided a substantial degree of scope not just for academic reflection but also for professional or practice-based reflection, particularly around subjects such as social change, discretion, professionalism and ethics.

Police roles, police cultures and wider society

Many of the more critical commentaries surrounding police work position policing as operating in a form of cultural vacuum. Policing is essentially portrayed as a societal role that is somehow distinct and separate from traditional society, with its practitioners adopting values that are fundamentally opposed to those held by wider society. In proposing such a viewpoint, it becomes obvious that police officers are sometimes depicted as two-dimensional caricatures in much the same ways that their detractors see the police as treating members of particular communities. This directly relates to the concept, coined by David Sklansky (2007), of 'cognitive burn-in', whereby ideas about the nature of policing, and the people who do it, become accepted with little critical assessment of their validity.

Such views are driven by the traditional focus on the role of the police officer as being a law enforcement role, and this assumption has led to many of the descriptions of policing that have emerged over the years. Take the work of Jereome Skolnick (1994), whose ground-breaking research provided the conceptual blueprint for many of the later police studies that came after it. In particular, his description of the cultural orientation of the police officer (what he called the police 'working personality') is very much grounded in the interaction between three main factors – danger, authority and the need to appear efficient. Policing, as an occupation, undoubtedly holds a degree of potential danger and accordingly, the notion of danger is symbolically embedded in many aspects of the occupational culture. At the same time, the police have a degree of authority which is denied to the rest of us and which is a fundamental aspect of the role. Finally, the need to 'get the job done' and to be efficient is, likewise, a central element of the role. Indeed, one could argue that this final element has grown in its importance since the 1980s, especially within the UK context.

However, Skolnick's model, for all of its strengths, fails to reflect the reality of what policing entails. In particular, as numerous commentators have suggested, police work is also shaped by its service role. To return to Sklansky's idea of 'cognitive burn-in', it appears that, to some observers, the police role is essentially a law enforcement role, and it is this over-simplification of the role of the police that may account for some of the deterministic and narrow accounts of police culture. At a more practical level, such assumptions can also influence the views of the communities that are policed and, importantly, the views that are held by police officers themselves. Arguably, therefore, it is unhelpful for police practitioners to adopt a similarly restricted view of their role. Evidence does appear to show that police officers are more likely to take a much broader view of the police role nowadays, and to perceive their role as driven by service, as well as law enforcement, values. The work of Sarah Charman (2017), in particular, highlights that more recent police recruits appear to have adopted cultural values that contradict those of officers who joined in previous generations. She suggests, for example, that today's new officers are much more likely to see their role in terms of safeguarding vulnerable populations. Furthermore, they increasingly tend to prioritise skills of effective communication. This contrasts starkly with the traditional perceptions that many hold about police culture. Today's practitioners might find it helpful, therefore, to reflect on what our knowledge here tells us about the accuracy of public perceptions of police work and also, the challenges of balancing a role that incorporates the two sometimes contradictory roles of law enforcement and service provision.

Similarly, we can further explore the perception that police culture refers to sets of assumptions, values and behaviours that lie beyond the realm of wider social culture. While much of the earlier research undertaken into police culture did not explicitly support such a viewpoint, increasingly the work of writers like Janet Chan (1997) suggests that external forces can shape the culture of the police and, furthermore, that individual police officers have agency (that is, can act independently and make their own choices). Such a position is interesting in that it suggests that there is not necessarily an enormous cultural divide between the outside world and that of the police as officers are now drawn from an ever larger section of the wider population. While it may have traditionally been the case that police culture reflected the broader characteristics of white working-class culture, it now seems that it increasingly accommodates a more complex array of assumptions and values that reflect the wider demographic from which the police are drawn. As a result, police practitioners might wish to compare the literature of police culture to their own experiences and to consider the ways in which it reflects the values of particular groups in society.

To conclude this particular section, it is appropriate to consider the extent to which police culture is, or should be, considered in negative terms. What is meant here is that police culture is generally viewed as being associated with a range of negative values (see, for example, the overview in Cockcroft, 2013) that lead to poor police practice. However, there is evidence to suggest that this is not wholly accurate. For example, the HMIC (1999) wisely noted that those officers whose work is lauded by the community and nominated for community awards belong to the same culture as those who act unprofessionally. How, then, do we account for such differences? Is this, again, due to the 'cognitive burn-in' (Sklansky, 2007) that directs us to view policing in terms of rigid stereotypes? One exercise that might be helpful here is for practitioners to reflect on the three layers that Edgar Schein (2004) identified as constituting organisational culture. To recap, these are shared assumptions (those usually unspoken assumptions that have become embedded as 'truth' among the cultural group), values (more conscious understandings of the world) and finally, artefacts (visible manifestations of underlying assumptions and values).

Professionalisation, discretion and ethics

While the above section has identified some areas for reflection around understanding what police culture is, this section will explore what police officers do, in an operational sense, and how best to understand the ways in which context impacts on this. Increasingly, as argued earlier in this book, it can be suggested that the police, as an institution, is becoming ever more focused on the ways in which police culture can lead to poor police practice (this is especially evident in the College of Policing's *Leadership Review*, 2015). While the extent to which the police culture (and its artefacts) can be viewed as wholly negative is debatable, this perception has led to initiatives that focus on the ways in which the discretionary elements of police work can lead to poor police practice. Once again, we find ourselves addressing the issue of discretion, and practitioners should be encouraged to reflect on the role that discretion plays in their professional practice, and the extent to which they feel that discretion is derived from the culture of their workplace or profession, the legislation that they enforce or the organisational procedures they follow. Similarly, practitioners may wish to consider the consequences for their working practices of both reductions, and increases, in their discretionary powers.

The College of Policing's *Code of Ethics* (2014) provides guidance on both the principles that should inform police decision-making and the standards expected of police officers. One of the purposes of the Code is to positively influence the ways in which officers exercise discretion. In particular, it advises that, while discretion is an inevitable facet of the police role, it needs to be exercised responsibly. The Code goes on to advise that discretion should be exercised in ways that reflect an officer's training, be consistent with policies and procedures, be based on consideration of outcomes and be consistent with the *Code of Ethics*. While obviously a response to the idea that police officers often act in ways that reflect the values of the police culture rather than the police organisation itself, this Code, although difficult to enforce, does provide some welcome guidance. This is most notable in respect of those principles that should be drawn on to guide the exercise of discretion. There does remain a challenge, however, that while the principles of the Code do present some worthy and appropriate aspirations, these concepts might be so vague as to have limited applicability to operational policing without some form of contextual inputs. For those who currently practise policing, these guidelines for practice do provide some scope for reflective exercise. First, it would be interesting to see if officers can identify any situations where the principles are difficult to abide by or where the principle of, for example, 'accountability' clashes with that of 'leadership'. Policing remains a conflicting and sometimes contradictory endeavour, and the application of abstract principles to real-world policing situations might generate interesting discussions around the Code, police culture and the tensions inherent to the police role.

These issues of professionalisation and ethics are very much tied to wider concerns regarding police legitimacy. While some of the more critical commentaries on policing identify a police culture that is fundamentally at odds with the values of wider society, another view can be taken that sees a lack of consensus in society. This leads us to identify a plurality of interests within society where the police reflect some of that society's values and not others, an inevitability in late-modern society. Furthermore, academic and police accounts both point to the suggestion that the police do reflect the interests of the societies in which they occur. To the academic John Crank (1998: 208), the police were 'a social and moral barometer of the society they inhabited'. Similarly, Sir Robert Mark, former Commissioner of the Metropolitan Police, noted that 'We, the police, are in fact the most accurate reflection of British society, its tolerance, its strengths and its weaknesses' (Mark, 1978: 33). While such reflections make little reference to the lack of consensus that characterises current society, they do, however, suggest that the police have, at a general level, the approval of some parts of society. Furthermore, as the work of Malcolm Sparrow et al (1990) shows, even unethical police behaviour, for example in respect of police use of unauthorised force, continues to exist in part because of the tacit approval of such behaviours by some elements of the public. Where this offers some scope for professional reflection is around how officers perceive the expectations of the public and how the public's idea of what policing is, and what it should be, compares to the professional standards expected of the police organisation. The *Code of Ethics* is of interest here in that it adopts a position that not only articulates what the generic police standards are but also in that it positions the standards of policing expected by the public as synonymous with those of the occupation's professional body. Readers may wish to reflect on how accurate they believe this assertion to be.

One of the central developments represented by the *Code of Ethics* can be found under Section 10 of the *Standards of Professional Behaviour*, 'Challenging and Reporting Improper Conduct'. While the Code's predominant focus is on the standards that police officers are required to adopt and abide by for their own practice, Section 10 identifies officers' obligations in responding to the behaviours of others. It states:

> According to this standard you must never ignore unethical or unprofessional behaviour by a policing colleague, irrespective of the person's rank, grade or role.... You have a positive obligation to question the conduct of colleagues that you believe falls below the expected standards and, if necessary, challenge, report or take action against such conduct. (College of Policing, 2014: 15)

This can be viewed as an attempt by the College of Policing to meet head on the concerns that police culture is one of the key obstacles to police professionalism through not only its ability to make certain behaviours appear appropriate but also through the unwritten principle that police officers should never report a colleague's behaviour to a superior, regardless of the nature of that behaviour. This might well be viewed as an attack on the camaraderie that is viewed as integral to the cultural world of the police officer, and raises the considerable question of, according to Louise Westmarland and Michael Rowe (2018: 867), 'will culture eat strategy for breakfast?' In other words, if the culture is directly targeted by a strategic intervention like this, which side will prevail? A point of reflection here for practitioners is to consider how they feel about this obligation to report colleagues who transgress the standards, and what factors they would take into account when deciding to either report or not to report them.

A final point to be made here regarding the ways in which police practitioners can understand police culture in relation to their professional practice is in respect of the increasingly fluid way in which we understand culture and its relationship with the concept of 'communities of practice' (see, for example, Wenger, 1998). Traditional conceptions of police culture can be viewed as deterministic in that they portray a relatively static and unchanging set of assumptions, values and behaviours that provide a very restricted range of options of police behaviours. As practitioners will no doubt recognise, policing is a more complex endeavour than such straightforward depictions allow for. From an academic viewpoint, Janet Chan's (1997) work allows us to rethink police culture and its relationship with those who undertake it by highlighting its fluidity and its relationship with external forces and by alerting us to the fact that individual officers are not merely unthinking vessels who gradually 'accumulate' their occupational culture as they experience the work environment of policing. As a result, this approach allows us to view culture as something that can also, under the right conditions, facilitate professionalisation. The work of Richard Heslop (2011) reminds us that experiential learning is an integral element of the skills acquisition of police officers, yet much of the discourse surrounding police culture positions this as a fundamental obstacle to professionalisation. The element of interactive peer-level socialisation present in the skills and knowledge base of police work does, arguably, link very closely to the concept of 'communities of practice'. This, according to Peter Jarvis (2007), refers to the ways in which active membership of communities (be they occupational or otherwise) are directly connected to the development of skills, knowledge and cultural capital. Once again, practitioners might wish to reflect on the extent to which their own experiences support, or refute, this idea.

References

Ainsworth, P.B. (2002) *Psychology and Policing*, Cullompton: Willan.

Asch, S. (1951) 'Effects of group pressure on the modification and distortion of judgements', in H. Guetzow (ed) *Groups, Leadership and Men*, Pittsburgh, PA: Carnegie, pp 177–90.

Babül, E. (2017) 'Morality: Understanding police training on human rights (Turkey)', in D. Fassin (ed) *Writing the World of Policing: The Difference Ethnography Makes*, Chicago, IL: University of Chicago Press, pp 139–61.

Bacon, M. (2014) 'Police culture and the new policing context', in J. Brown (ed) *The Future of Policing*, London: Routledge, pp 103–19.

Balenovich, J., Grossi, E. and Hughes, T. (2008) 'Toward a balanced approach: Defining police roles in responding to domestic violence', *American Journal of Criminal Justice*, 33(1): 19–31.

Ballucci, D., Gill, C. and Campbell, M.A. (2017) 'The power of attitude: The role of police culture and receptivity of risk assessment tools in IPV calls', *Policing: A Journal of Policy and Practice*, 11(3): 242–57.

Banakar, R. and Travers, M. (2005) 'Introduction', in R. Banakar and M. Travers (eds) *Theory and Method in Socio-Legal Research*, Oxford: Hart, pp ix–xvi.

Bass, B.M. and Avolio, B.J. (1993) 'Transformational leadership and organizational culture', *Public Administration Quarterly*, 17: 112–22.

BBC News (2018) 'Lincolnshire Police facing "significant cuts to services"', [online] 24 November, Available from: www.bbc.co.uk/news/uk-england-lincolnshire-45641887 (accessed 31 November 2018).

Beck, U. (1992) *Risk Society: Towards a New Modernity*, London: Sage.

Becker, H. (1963) *Outsiders*, New York: Free Press.

Berger, P.L. and Luckmann, T. (1966) *The Social Construction of Reality*, Harmondsworth: Penguin Books.

Beynon, H. (1984) *Working for Ford*, Harmondsworth: Penguin Books.

Beynon, H. (2011) 'Engaging Labour: British sociology 1945–2010', *Global Labour Journal*, 2(1): 5–26.

Blumer, H. (1969) *Symbolic Interactionism*, Englewood Cliffs, NJ: Prentice-Hall.

Bohannan, P. (1965) 'The differing realms of the law', *American Anthropologist*, 67(6): 33–42.

Bowling, B. and Phillips, C. (2003) 'Policing ethnic minority communities', in T. Newburn (ed) *Handbook of Policing*, Cullompton: Willan, pp 528–55.

Bowling, B., Parmar, A. and Phillips, C. (2008) 'Policing minority ethnic communities', in T. Newburn (ed) *Handbook of Policing* (2nd edn), Cullompton: Willan, pp 611–41.

Brogden, M. (1982) *The Police: Autonomy and Consent*, London: Academic Press.

Brogden, M. (1991) *On the Mersey Beat: An Oral History of Policing Liverpool Between the Wars*, Oxford: Oxford University Press.

Brogden, M., Jefferson, T. and Walklate, S. (1988) *Introducing Policework*, London: Unwin Hyman.

Brown, J. (2007) 'From cult of masculinity to smart macho: Gender perspectives on police occupational culture', in M. O'Neill, M. Marks and A. Singh (eds) *Police Occupational Culture: New Debates and Directions*, New York: Elsevier, pp 205–26.

Burton Jr, V.S., Frank, J., Langworthy, R.H. and Barker, T.A. (1993) 'The prescribed roles of police in a free society: Analyzing state legal codes', *Justice Quarterly*, 10(4): 683–95.

Butterfield, R., Edwards, C. and Woodall, J. (2005) 'The new public management and managerial roles: The case of the police sergeant', *British Journal of Management*, 16(4): 329–41.

Cain, M. (1973) *Society and the Policeman's Role*, London: Routledge and Kegan Paul.

Caless, B. (2011) *Policing at the Top*, Bristol: Policy Press.

Campeau, H. (2015) 'Police culture at work: Making sense of police oversight', *British Journal of Criminology*, 55(4): 669–87.

Carlson, H.M. and Sutton, M.S. (1974) 'The development of attitudes as a function of police roles', *Proceedings of the Division of Personality and Society Psychology*, 1(1): 113–15.

Chan, J. (1997) *Changing Police Culture: Policing in a Multicultural Society*, Cambridge: Cambridge University Press.

Charman, S. (2017) *Police Socialisation, Identity and Culture*, London: Palgrave Macmillan.

Cockcroft, T. (2001) 'An investigation into the culture of the London Metropolitan Police between the 1930s and the 1960s', Unpublished PhD thesis, Uxbridge: Brunel University.

Cockcroft, T. (2005) 'Using oral history to investigate police culture', *Qualitative Research*, 5(3): 365–84.

Cockcroft, T. (2007) 'Police culture(s): Some definitional, contextual and analytical considerations', in M. O'Neill, M. Marks and A. Singh (eds) *Police Occupational Culture: New Debates and Directions*, New York: Elsevier, pp 85–102.

Cockcroft, T. (2010) 'Vers une reconnaissance de la valeur de l'histoire orale de la police en criminologie', in J. Berlière and R. Lévy (eds) *L'Historien, le Sociologue et le Témoin. Archives Orales et Récits de Vie: Usages et Problèmes*, Paris: Nouveau Monde Éditions, pp 241–60.

Cockcroft, T. (2013) *Police Culture: Themes and Concepts*, London: Routledge.

Cockcroft, T. (2014) 'Police culture and transformational leadership: Outlining the contours of a troubled relationship', *Policing: A Journal of Policy and Practice*, 8(1): 5–13.

Cockcroft, T. (2015) 'Golden ages, red herrings and post-Keynesian policing: Understanding the role of police culture in the police professionalism debate', *Nordic Journal of Studies in Policing*, 2(2): 183–96.

Cockcroft, T. (2017) 'Police culture: Histories, orthodoxies, and new horizons', *Policing: A Journal of Policy and Practice*, 11(3): 229–35.

Cockcroft, T. (2019) 'Police culture and police leadership', in P. Ramshaw, M. Silvestri and M. Simpson (eds) *Leadership in Policing: Changing Landscapes*, London: Palgrave Macmillan, pp 23–45.

Cockcroft, T. and Beattie, I. (2009) 'Shifting cultures: Managerialism and the rise of "performance"', *Policing: An International Journal of Police Strategies and Management*, 32(3): 526–40.

Cockcroft, T., Shan-A-Khuda, M., Schreuders, C. and Trevorrow, P. (2018) 'Police cybercrime training: Perceptions, pedagogy and policy', *Policing: A Journal of Policy and Practice*, Available from: https://doi.org/10.1093/police/pay078

College of Policing (no date) *Resources for Reflective Practice*, London: College of Policing, Available from: www.college.police.uk/What-we-do/Development/professional-development-programme/Documents/Resources_for_reflective_practice_v1_0.pdf (accessed 27 February 2019).

College of Policing (2014) *Code of Ethics: A Code of Practice for the Principles and Standards of Professional Behaviour for the Policing Profession of England and Wales*, London: College of Policing.

College of Policing (2015) *Leadership Review: Recommendations for Delivering Leadership at All Levels*, London: College of Policing, Available from: www.college.police.uk/What-we-do/Development/Promotion/the-leadership-review/Documents/Leadership_Review_Final_June-2015.pdf (accessed 27 September 2017).

Collins, P.A. and Gibbs, A.C.C. (2003) 'Stress in police officers: A study of the origins, prevalence and severity of stress-related symptoms within a county police force', *Occupational Medicine*, 53(4): 256–64.

Crank, J.P. (1998) *Understanding Police Culture*, Cincinnati, OH: Anderson.

Davis, K.C. (1969) *Discretionary Justice*, Baton Rouge, LA: Louisiana State University Press.

Davis, K.C. (1975) *Police Discretion*, St Paul, MN: West.

Deissinger, T. (2004) 'Apprenticeship systems in England and Germany: Decline and survival', in W. Greinert and G. Hanf (eds) *Towards a History of Vocational Education and Training (VET) in Europe in a Comparative Perspective: First International Conference 2002*, Florence: Luxembourg: Office for Official Publications of the European Communities, pp 28–45.

de Maillard, J. and Savage, S.P. (2018) 'Policing as a performing art? The contradictory nature of contemporary police performance management', *Criminology and Criminal Justice*, 18(3): 314–31.

Densten, I.L. (1999) 'Senior Australian law enforcement leadership under examination', *Policing: An International Journal of Police Strategies and Management*, 22(1): 45–57.

Dodd, V. and Stratton, A. (2011) 'Bill Bratton says he can lead police out of "crisis" despite budget cuts', *The Guardian*, [online] 14 August, Available from: www.guardian.co.uk/uk/2011/aug/14/bill-bratton-police-crisis-cuts (accessed 26 February 2012).

Duncan, B. (1976) 'Differential social perception and attribution of intergroup violence: Testing the lower limits of stereotyping blacks', *Journal of Personality and Social Psychology*, 34(4): 590–8.

Dunham, R.G. and Petersen, N. (2017) 'Making black lives matter: Evidence-based policies for reducing police bias in the use of deadly force', *Criminology and Public Policy*, 16(1): 341–8.

Durão, S. (2017) 'Detention: Police discretion revisited (Portugal)', in D. Fassin (ed) *Writing the World of Policing: The Difference Ethnography Makes*, Chicago, IL: University of Chicago Press, pp 225–47.

Elliot, D., Garg, B., Kuehl, K., DeFrancesco, C. and Sleigh, A. (2015) 'Why are women law enforcement officers more burned-out and what might help them?', *Occupational Medicine & Health Affairs*, 3(3): 1–4.

Emsley, C. (1991) *The English Police: A Political and Social History*, London: Harvester Wheatsheaf.

Emsley, C. (2008) 'The birth and development of the police', in T. Newburn (ed) *Handbook of Policing* (2nd edn), Cullompton: Willan, pp 72–89.

Enloe, C.H. (1976) 'Ethnicity and militarization: Factors shaping the roles of police in third world nations', *Studies in Comparative International Development*, 11(3): 25–38.

Eraut, M. (2000) 'Non-formal learning and tacit knowledge in professional work', *British Journal of Educational Psychology*, 70(1): 113–36.

Evetts, J. (2013) 'Professionalism: Value and ideology', *Current Sociology*, 61(5–6): 778–96.

Fairhurst, G. and Grant, D. (2010) 'The social construction of leadership: A sailing guide', *Management Communication Quarterly*, 24(2): 171–210.

Fassin, D. (ed) (2017a) *Writing the World of Policing: The Difference Ethnography Makes*, Chicago, IL: University of Chicago Press.

Fassin, D. (2017b) 'Ethnographying the police', in D. Fassin (ed) *Writing the World of Policing: The Difference Ethnography Makes*, Chicago, IL: University of Chicago Press, pp 1–20.

Fassin, D. (2017c) 'Boredom: Accounting for the ordinary in the work of policing (France)', in D. Fassin (ed) *Writing the World of Policing: The Difference Ethnography Makes*, Chicago, IL: University of Chicago Press, pp 269–92.

Festinger, L. (1954) 'A theory of social comparison processes', *Human Relations*, 7(2): 117–40.

FitzGerald, M., Hough, M., Joseph, I. and Qureshi, T. (2002) *Policing for London*, Cullompton: Willan.

Flanagan, R. (2008) *The Review of Policing: Final Report*, London: HMSO.

Foster, J. (1989) 'Two stations: An ethnographic study of policing in the inner city', in D. Downes (ed) *Crime and the City*, London: Macmillan, pp 128–53.

Foster, J. (2003) 'Police cultures', in T. Newburn (ed) *Handbook of Policing*, Cullompton: Willan, pp 196–227.

Fournier, V. (1999) 'The appeal to "professionalism" as a disciplinary mechanism', *The Sociological Review*, 47(2): 280–307.

Fox, J.C. and Lundman, R.J. (1974) 'Problems and strategies in gaining research access in police organizations', *Criminology*, 12(1): 52–69.

Fyfe, N. (2017) 'Evidence based policing', in *Policing 2026 Evidence Review*, Dundee: SIPR (Scottish Institute for Policing Research), pp 9–19.

Garland, D. (2001) *The Culture of Control*, Oxford: Oxford University Press.

Girodo, M. (1998) 'Machiavellian, bureaucratic, and transformational leadership styles in police managers: Preliminary findings of interpersonal ethics', *Perceptual and Motor Skills*, 86(2): 419–27.

Golding, B. and Savage, S.P. (2008) 'Leadership and performance management', in T. Newburn (ed) *Handbook of Policing* (2nd edn), Cullompton: Willan, pp 725–59.

Goode, J. and Lumsden, K. (2018) 'The McDonaldisation of police–academic partnerships: Organisational and cultural barriers encountered in moving from research on police to research with police', *Policing and Society*, 28(1): 75–89.

Gregory, K.L. (1983) 'Native-view paradigms: Multiple cultures and culture conflicts in organizations', *Administrative Science Quarterly*, 28(3): 359–76.

Grint, K and Thornton, S. (2015) 'Leadership, management and command in the police', in J. Fleming (ed) *Police Leadership: Rising to the Top*, Oxford: Oxford University Press, pp 95–109.

Hallenberg, K. (2012) 'Scholarly detectives: Police professionalisation via academic education', Unpublished PhD thesis, Manchester: University of Manchester.

Hallenberg, K. and Cockcroft, T. (2017) 'From indifference to hostility: Police officers, organisational responses and the symbolic value of "in-service" higher education in policing', *Policing: A Journal of Policy and Practice*, 11(3): 273–88.

Harvey, D. (2007) *A Brief History of Neoliberalism*, Oxford: Oxford University Press.

Heidensohn, F. (1985) *Women and Crime*, Basingstoke: Macmillan.

Heidensohn, F. (2008) 'Gender and policing', in T. Newburn (ed) *Handbook of Policing* (2nd edn), Cullompton: Willan, pp 642–65.

Herbert, S. (2017) 'Accountability: Ethnographic engagement and the ethics of the police (United States)', in D. Fassin (ed) *Writing the World of Policing: The Difference Ethnography Makes*, Chicago, IL: University of Chicago Press, pp 23–41.

Heslop, R. (2011) 'Community engagement and learning as "becoming": Findings from a study of British police recruit training', *Policing and Society*, 21(3): 327–42.

HMIC (Her Majesty's Inspectorate of Constabulary) (1999) *Winning the Race – Revisited: A Follow Up to the HMIC Thematic Inspection Report on Police Community and Race Relations (1998/1999)*, London: HMSO.

HMIC (2014) *Everyone's Business: Improving the Police Response to Domestic Abuse*, London: HMIC, Available from: www.justiceinspectorates.gov.uk/hmicfrs/wp-content/uploads/2014/04/improving-the-police-response-to-domestic-abuse.pdf (accessed 27 February 2019).

HMIC (2015) *Real Lives, Real Crimes: A Study of Digital Crime and Policing*, London: HMIC.

Hobbs, D. (1988) *Doing the Business: Entrepreneurship, Detectives and the Working Class in the East End of London*, Oxford: Clarendon.

Home Office (1983) 'Manpower, Effectiveness and Efficiency in the Police Service', Circular 114/83, London: Home Office.

House of Commons Library (2018) 'Police numbers in England & Wales', Available from: https://researchbriefings.parliament. uk/ResearchBriefing/Summary/SN02615#fullreport (accessed 28 February 2019).

Innes, M. (2010) 'The art, craft and science of policing', in P. Cane and H.M. Kritzer (eds) *The Handbook of Empirical Legal Research*, Oxford: Oxford University Press, pp 11–36.

Jarvis, P. (2007) *Globalisation, Lifelong Learning and the Learning Society*, Abingdon: Routledge.

Jefferson, M. (2009) *Criminal Law* (9th edn), London: Pearson.

Jones, T. and Newburn, T. (2002) 'The transformation of policing? Understanding current trends in policing systems', *British Journal of Criminology*, 42(1): 129–46.

Kaplan-Lyman, J. (2012) 'A punitive bind: Policing, poverty, and neoliberalism in New York City', *Yale Human Rights and Development Law Journal*, 15(1): 177–221.

Keane, J. and Bell, P. (2014) 'Ethics and police management: The impact of leadership style on misconduct by senior police leaders in the United Kingdom and Australia', *International Journal of Management and Administrative Sciences*, 2(3): 1–15.

Klockars, C. (1985) *The Idea of Police*, Beverly Hills, CA: Sage.

Krimmel, J.T. and Lindenmuth, P. (2001) 'Police chief performance and leadership styles', *Police Quarterly*, 4(4): 469–83.

Kyed, H.M. (2017) 'Predicament: Interpreting police violence (Mozambique)', in D. Fassin (ed) *Writing the World of Policing: The Difference Ethnography Makes*, Chicago, IL: University of Chicago Press, pp 113–38.

LaFave, W. (1962) 'The police and nonenforcement of the law – Part ii', *Wisconsin Law Review*, 179–239.

Loader, I. and Mulcahy, A. (2003) *Policing and the Condition of England: Memory, Politics and Culture*, Oxford: Oxford University Press.

Loftus, B. (2009) *Police Culture in a Changing World*, Oxford: Oxford University Press.

Loftus, B. (2010) 'Police occupational culture: Classic themes, altered times', *Policing and Society*, 20(1): 1–20.

Long, L. and Joseph-Salisbury, R. (2019) 'Black mixed-race men's perceptions and experiences of the police', *Ethnic and Racial Studies*, 42(2): 198–215.

Lum, C. and Koper, C.S. (2014) 'Evidence-based policing', in G. Bruinsma and D. Weisburd (eds) *Encyclopedia of Criminology and Criminal Justice*, New York: Springer, pp 1426–37.

Macpherson, W. (1999) *The Stephen Lawrence Inquiry*, Cm 4262, London: HMSO.

Magenau, J.M. and Hunt, R.G. (1989) 'Sociopolitical networks for police role-making', *Human Relations*, 42(6): 547–60.

Maguire, M. (2008) 'Criminal investigation and crime control', in T. Newburn (ed) *Handbook of Policing* (2nd edn), Cullompton: Willan, pp 430–64.

Maguire, M. and Norris, C. (1994) 'Police investigations: Practice and malpractice', *Journal of Law and Society*, 21: 72–84.

Malinowski, B. (2005) *Argonauts of the Western Pacific: An Account of Native Enterprise and Adventure in the Archipelagoes of Melanesian New Guinea*, London: Taylor and Francis.

Manning, P.K. (1977) *Police Work: The Social Organization of Policing*, Cambridge, MA: MIT.

Manning, P.K. (1989) 'Occupational culture', in W.G. Bailey (ed) *The Encyclopedia of Police Science*, New York: Garland, pp 360–3.

Manning, P.K. (1993) 'Toward a theory of police organization polarities and change', Paper to the International Conference on 'Social Change and Policing', 3–5 August, Taipei.

Manning, P.K. (2007) 'A dialectic of organisational and occupational culture' in M. O'Neill, M. Marks and A. Singh (eds) *Police Occupational Culture: New Debates and Directions*, London: Elsevier, pp 47–83.

Mark, R. (1978) *In the Office of Constable*, London: Collins.

Marks, M. (2007) 'Police unions and their influence: Subculture or counter culture', in M. O'Neill, M. Marks and A. Singh (eds) *Police Occupational Culture: New Debates and Directions*, New York: Elsevier, pp 229–51.

McLaughlin, E. (2007) *The New Policing*, London: Sage.

Metropolitan Police Federation (2015) '#CutsHaveConsequences update', [online] 19 February, Available from: www.metfed.org.uk/cuts-have-consequences (accessed 3 March 2019).

Newburn, T. (2008) 'Policing since 1945', in T. Newburn (ed) *Handbook of Policing* (2nd edn), Cullompton: Willan, pp 90–114.

Neyroud, P. (2008) 'Ethics in policing', in T. Newburn and P. Neyroud (eds) *Dictionary of Policing*, Cullompton: Willan, pp 97–8.

Niederhoffer, A. (1969) *Behind the Shield: The Police in Urban Society*, New York: Anchor.

Nishida, H. (1999) 'Cultural schema theory', in W.B. Gudykunst (ed) *Theorizing About Intercultural Communication*, Thousand Oaks, CA: Sage, pp 401–18.

O'Malley, P. and Hutchinson, S. (2007) 'Converging corporatization? Police management, police unionism, and the transfer of business principles', *Police Practice and Research*, 8(2): 159–74.

O'Neill, M. and Holdaway, S. (2007) 'Black police associations and the police occupational culture', in M. O'Neill, M. Marks and A. Singh (eds) *Police Occupational Culture: New Debates and Directions*, New York: Elsevier, pp 253–74.

Paoline, E.A. (2003) 'Taking stock: Towards a richer understanding of police culture', *Journal of Criminal Justice*, 31(3): 199–214.

Pelfrey Jr, W.V. (2004) 'The inchoate nature of community policing: Differences between community policing and traditional police officers', *Justice Quarterly*, 21(3): 579–601.

Punch, M. (1979) 'The secret social service', in S. Holdaway (ed) *The British Police*, London: Edward Arnold, pp 102–17.

QAA (Quality Assurance Agency for Higher Education) (2014) *Subject Benchmark Statement: Criminology*, Gloucester: QAA.

Rawlings, P. (2002) *Policing: A Short History*, Cullompton: Willan.

Ray, R., Brown, M., Fraistat, N. and Summers, E. (2017) 'Ferguson and the death of Michael Brown on Twitter: #BlackLivesMatter, #TCOT, and the evolution of collective identities', *Ethnic and Racial Studies*, 40(11): 1797–813.

Reiner, R. (1992a) *The Politics of the Police* (2nd edn), London: Harvester Wheatsheaf.

Reiner, R. (1992b) *Chief Constables*, Oxford: Oxford University Press.

Reiner, R. (2010) *The Politics of the Police* (4th edn), Oxford: Oxford University Press.

Reiner, R. and Newburn, T. (2007) 'Police research', in R.D. King and E. Wincup (eds) *Doing Research on Crime and Justice* (2nd edn), Oxford: Oxford University Press, pp 343–74.

Reuss-Ianni, E. and Ianni, F. (1983) 'Street cops and management cops: The two cultures of policing', in M. Punch (ed) *Control in the Police Organization*, Cambridge, MA: MIT, pp 251–74.

Robinson, A.L. (2000) 'The effect of a domestic violence policy change on police officers' schemata', *Criminal Justice and Behavior*, 27(5): 600–24.

Roszak, T. (1995) *The Making of a Counter Culture*, Berkeley, CA: University of California Press.

Rowe, M. (2006) 'Following the leader: Front-line narratives on police leadership', *Policing: An International Journal of Police Strategies and Management*, 29(4): 757–67.

Rufo, R.A. (2016) 'Welcome to the police academy', in R.A. Rufo (ed) *Police Suicide: Is Police Culture Killing Our Officers?*, Boca Raton, FL: CRC Press, pp 1–20.

Scarman, G. (1982) *The Scarman Report: The Brixton Disorders 10–12 April 1981*, London: Pelican.

Schein, E. (2004) *Organizational Culture and Leadership* (3rd edn), San Francisco, CA: Jossey-Bass.

Sewell, J.D. (1983) 'The development of a critical life events scale for law enforcement', *Journal of Police Science and Administration*, 11(1): 113–14.

Shearing, C. and Ericson, R.V. (1991) 'Culture as figurative action', *British Journal of Sociology*, 42(4): 481–506.

Sheehy Report (1993) *Report of the Inquiry into Police Responsibilities and Rewards*, Cm 2280, I, II, London: HMSO.

Sherman, L. (1982) 'Learning police ethics', *Criminal Justice Ethics*, 1(1): 10–19.

Sherman, L. (1998) *Evidence-Based Policing*, Ideas in American Policing Series, Washington, DC: Police Foundation.

Sherman, L. (2013) 'The rise of evidence-based policing: Targeting, testing, and tracking', *Crime and Justice*, 42(1): 377–451.

Silvestri, M. (2007) '"Doing" police leadership: Enter the "new smart macho"', *Policing and Society*, 17(1): 38–58.

Silvestri, M. (2003) *Women in Charge: Policing, Gender and Leadership*, Cullompton: Willan.

Silvestri, M. (2015) 'Gender diversity: Two steps forward, one step back...', *Policing: A Journal of Policy and Practice*, 9(1): 56–64.

Silvestri, M. (2017) 'Police culture and gender: Revisiting the "cult of masculinity"', *Policing: A Journal of Policy and Practice*, 11(3): 289–300.

Skidelsky, R. (1975) *Oswald Mosley*, London: Macmillan.

Sklansky, D.A. (2007) 'Seeing blue: Police reform, occupational culture, and cognitive burn-in', in M. O'Neill, M. Marks and A. Singh (eds) *Police Occupational Culture: New Debates and Directions*, New York: Elsevier, pp 19–45.

Sklansky, D. (2014) 'The promise and perils of police professionalism', in J. Brown (ed) *The Future of Policing*, London: Routledge, pp 373–84.

Skolnick, J.H. (1994) *Justice Without Trial: Law Enforcement in Democratic Society* (3rd edn), London: Wiley.

Skolnick, J.H. (2007) 'Racial profiling – then and now', *Criminology & Public Policy*, 6(1): 65–70.

Smith, D. and Gray, J. (1983) *Police and People in London, Vol 4: The Police in Action*, London: Policy Studies Institute.

Song Richardson, L. (2014) 'Police racial violence: Lessons from social psychology', *Fordham Law Review*, 83: 2961–76.

Sparrow, M.K., Moore, M.H. and Kennedy, D.M. (1990) *Beyond 911: A New Era for Policing*, New York: Basic Books.

Storch, R. (1976) 'The policeman as domestic missionary: Urban discipline and popular culture in Northern England 1850–1880', *Journal of Social History*, 9(4): 481–509.

Summerfield, D. (2011) 'Metropolitan Police blues: Protracted sickness absence, ill health retirement, and the occupational psychiatrist', *British Medical Journal*, 342: 950–2.

Terpstra, J. (2017) 'Storytelling about rural policing – The social construction of a professional identity', *European Journal of Police Studies*, 4(4): 17–33.

Terpstra, J. and van der Vijver, K. (2006) 'The police, changing security arrangements and late modernity: The case of the Netherlands', *German Policy Studies*, 3(1): 80.

Tong, S., Bryant, R.P. and Horvath, M.A. (2009) *Understanding Criminal Investigation*, Chichester: John Wiley & Sons.

Touraine, A. (1989) 'Is sociology still the study of society?', *Thesis Eleven*, 23(1): 5–34.

Tsoukas, H. (1997) 'The tyranny of light: The temptations and the paradoxes of the information society', *Futures*, 29(9): 827–43.

Tyler, T.R. (1990) *Why People Obey the Law*, New Haven, CT: Yale University Press.

van Hulst, M. (2014) 'Police officers telling stories', British Society of Criminology Newsletter, No 75 (Winter), pp 14–15, Available from: http://britsoccrim.org/new/newdocs/bscn-75-2014_vanhulst.pdf (accessed 18 July 2018).

van Maanen, J. (1978a) 'On watching the watchers', in P. Manning and J. van Maanen (eds) *Policing: A View from the Street*, Santa Monica, CA: Goodyear, pp 309–49.

van Maanen, J. (1978b) 'The asshole', in P. Manning and J. van Maanen (eds) *Policing: A View from the Street*, Santa Monica, CA: Goodyear, pp 221–38.

van Maanen, J. (1984) 'Making rank: Becoming an American police sergeant', *Urban Life*, 13(2): 155–76.

Venema, R.M. (2014) 'Police officer schema of sexual assault reports: Real rape, ambiguous cases, and false reports', *Journal of Interpersonal Violence*, 31(5): 872–99.

Waddington, P.A.J. (1998) *Policing Citizens*, London: UCL Press.

Waddington, P.A.J. (1999) 'Police (canteen) sub-culture: An appreciation', *British Journal of Criminology*, 39(2): 287–309.

Walklate, S. and Mythen, G. (2008) 'How scared are we?', *British Journal of Criminology*, 48(2): 209–25.

Weber, M. (1949) *The Methodology of the Social Sciences: A Selection and Translation of Essays*, translated by E. Shils and H.A. Finch, New York: Free Press.

Weinberger, B. (1995) *The Best Police in the World: An Oral History of English Policing*, Aldershot: Ashgate.

Wenger, E. (1998) *Communities of Practice*, Cambridge: Cambridge University Press.

Westmarland, L. (2001) *Gender and Policing: Sex, Power and Police Culture*, Cullompton: Willan.

Westmarland, L. (2005) 'Police ethics and integrity: Breaking the blue code of silence', *Policing and Society*, 15(2): 145–65.

Westmarland, L. (2017) 'Putting their bodies on the line: Police culture and gendered physicality', *Policing: A Journal of Policy and Practice*, 11(3): 301–17.

Westmarland, L. and Rowe, M. (2018) 'Police ethics and integrity: Can a new code overturn the blue code?', *Policing and Society*, 28(7): 854–70.

White, J. (1983) 'Police and people in London in the 1930s', *Oral History*, 11(2): 34–41.

Williams, E. and Cockcroft, T. (2019) 'Knowledge wars: professionalisation, organisational justice and competing knowledge paradigms in British policing', in L. Huey and R. Mitchell (eds) *Evidence-Based Policing: An Introduction*, Bristol: Policy Press, pp 131–41.

Wilson, J.Q. (1968) *Varieties of Police Behavior: The Management of Law and Order in Eight Communities*, Cambridge, MA: Harvard University Press.

Wolfenden, J. (1957) *Report of the Committee on Homosexual Offences and Prostitution*, Cm 247, London: HMSO.

Wood, D., Cockcroft, T., Tong, S. and Bryant, R. (2017) 'The importance of context and cognitive agency in developing police knowledge: Going beyond the police science discourse', *The Police Journal: Theory, Practice and Principles*, 91(2): 173–87.

Wrigley, E.A. (1990) *Continuity, Chance and Change: The Character of the Industrial Revolution in England*, Cambridge: Cambridge University Press.

Young, J. (2007) *The Vertigo of Late Modernity*, London: Sage.

Young, M. (1991) *An Inside Job*, Oxford: Clarendon.

Young, S. (2015) 'Policing "uncontrollable banshees": Factors influencing arrest decision making', *Safer Communities*, 14(4): 183–92.

Index